Praise for Ted Lerner's
Hey, Joe

"The American-born Lerner is well qualified to write about his corner of Asia, the Philippines... he offers some refreshingly non-judgmental insights..."   *-Far Eastern Economic Review*

"Love it or hate it, Manila ... is always ripe for anecdotes and wry observation. You'll find both of these in long time expatriate resident Ted Lerner's hilarious Hey, Joe ... the must read..."
-Business Traveller Asia-Pacific

"Lerner is at his best ... such as in the finely observed piece on the behind-the-scenes shenanigans that accompanied a 1995 international boxing bout."   *-South China Morning Post*

"I've found it exceedingly enjoyable, insightful, informative, and, at times, laugh-out-loud funny. Congratulations. I sincerely hope it is the first of many."   *-Ring Magazine, USA*

"...Lerner's humor easily shines through, making this anthology a must read not only for expats but also for Filipinos..."
-Manila Bulletin

"The book fascinated me and had me hooked..."
-Malaya Newspaper

"Lerner's at his best when he recounts his forays at the Balintawak market, the ways of the cheapo bars, the sliding scale of fortune-tellers' fees, or rites of passage involving the prizefighting business. He can be prolix, but often engaging. Absorbing, even."

-The Philippine Star

"Hey, Joe is probably one of the best books on Manila to come out of late. I hate to say this but it was a big plus that the author is American. Only with such detachment could this truly unique perspective have been captured on paper."   *-The Daily Tribune*

"Lerner seems to be equipped with extra sensitive senses and an acute power of observation that makes for very entertaining and articulate writing. "Hey, Joe" tackles the mundane, bizarre, amusing, macabre, and maddening aspects about life in Manila. Lerner comes across as truly interested, amazed, and fascinated through the easily neglected balut vendor, the omnipresent lugaw vendor, the cash strapped bar girl, the bustling Balint-awak Market and the sabungero (cock fight player). No detail seems to escape him. And neither does his sense of humor and childlike fascination."
                                            -The Manila Times

"The Yiddish Yank Ted Lerner has really pissed me off. We have been fellow scribes attempting to make a living in a world of 2 pesos a word. Because of this fact in life, we both had adopted the simple policy of never using 10 words when 100 were possible... Now Lerner has written his first book and I was asked to review it. Having just put it down, I am really pissed off because he has clearly shown that he has something that eludes myself—talent with a capital 'T.'"
                                            -The Foreign Post

"Lerner finds some kind of hidden magic in the nuances of every-day Pinoy life, magic that has long since vanished from Western living. His clean, friendly prose serves "Hey, Joe" well, acting as a magnet for those who want to see yet another version of Ma-nila—this one through the eyes of a besotted foreigner."
                                            -Philippine Daily Inquirer

"In his book, Lerner caricatures various Filipino characters that are so familiar, not because you know them in person but because you know that's how Filipinos are. And, after years abroad, you realize these are the people that make you dream of going back."
                                            -The Sun Hong Kong

Hey, Joe

a slice of the city —
an American in Manila...

TED LERNER

Corregidor Peace Institute Press
www.corregidorpeaceinstitute.org

Author:
TED LERNER
ted@hey-joe.net

Illustrator:
VICKY VILLANUEVA FIRESTONE

Copyright © 2007 by Ted Lerner

Published by the Corregidor Peace Institute Press (CPIP), Philippines, 2007
www.corregidorpeaceinstitute.org

Originally published by Book of Dreams Verlag, Germany, 1999
Back cover photo: Marcelline S. Santos

ISBN 978-971-93834-0-6
Printed in China

Distributor in the Philippines:
Asiatype Distribution Inc.
Ground Floor, Columbia Tower, Ortigas Avenue, Greenhills, Mandaluyong City
Tel.: 744-6262; Fax: 721-0383
E-mail: contact@asiatype-distribution.com
www.asiatype-distribution.com

to mom and pop,

for setting the stage.

ACKNOWLEDGMENT

Thanks must first go to my good buddy Richie, for insisting I visit the Philippines when I was terrified to go.

Also to my editors at BusinessWorld, Vladimir Bunoan and Lali Herrera, for offering me the space to print whatever story I want to tell.

And thanks to my wife Au (pronounced like OUch!), for being a sounding board on all things Filipino, for half the headlines that grace these stories, and, of course, for Shanti.

Thanks also to the friendly people who make up this extraordinary metropolis known as Metro Manila, for providing a curious foreigner a never ending welcome and a story around every corner.

CONTENTS

The American architect, Daniel Burnham, prepared the plan of the city (of Manila) in 1904. His plan had five interrelated components: (1) the development of the waterfront and the location of parks and parkways to give adequate recreation in every quarter of the city, (2) the establishment of a street system which would provide direct and easy connection to every point of the city, (3) the location of building sites for various activities, (4) the development of waterways for transportation, and (5) the provision of summer resorts.

But the city developed in a less orderly manner than the plan Burnham had laid down.

The World Book Encyclopedia

FOREWORD

When Ted Lerner asked me to write the foreword of this book you are now reading, it was almost like having your good pal ask you to be his best man. That's how it felt. It's both an honor and a responsibility, except that I don't have to plan his bachelor party.

We've talked about this book for quite some time now. Ted has always been keen on coming up with a compilation of his writing and we'd always argue on how he should go about it. I gave him the names of a couple of regional publishers that might be interested in such a project, notably the Singaporean group that came out with the Sarong Party Girl series, which I personally like. They exchanged correspondence but Ted was adamant about keeping the integrity of his work, and not changing it to suit the tastes of his prospective publishers. So that was that.

But that's Ted for you. Although he sometimes appears too forgiving and understanding of the zany, bizarre and often frustrating aspects of life in the Philippines, there is still a part of him that is idealistic. I recall receiving angry phone calls because of some typographical errors that were not corrected. Or if I change his given title. Or when I just totally disagree with what he has written. But after 10 minutes of listening to him scream at me over the phone, he'd forget about it.

I thought Ted had forgotten about this book project. We hadn't talked about it for quite some time until one day he called up and said he found a publisher. He had the green light. And he wanted me to write this.

It started, for me anyway, in Phuket, Thailand. I bought a local magazine published by an Australian expatriate which had a column called "The Ugly American." It was about the (mis)adventures of a foreigner in Thailand and it gave me a unique insight about the country which I wouldn't otherwise get in the usual travel book.

I remembered this column when I became the Arts & Leisure editor of BusinessWorld. I enthusiastically thought of new stuff I wanted to introduce to the section and one of them was a column just like "The Ugly American."

By that time, I had already read Ted Lerner, who was then writing a sports column for Expat newspaper. He was on top of my short list, especially after reading one column he wrote about a bus ride from Northern Luzon and where he had to endure six hours of Air Supply music. It was very observant, I thought, capturing the Filipino penchant for sentimental love songs, seamlessly woven with sports reportage.

The problem was he was with another paper, whose publisher is a friend of mine. I offered the column instead to Ted's former editor, a British chap who also has a very readable, witty style. He accepted but two weeks before the column was to debut, he begged from the task as he had suddenly become very busy in his job. He added quickly though that Ted had left Expat and gave me his number.

I called Ted and pitched the idea and set an appointment to meet at the Beverly Hills Deli in Greenbelt. I brought a copy of "The Ugly American" for him to give him an idea of how the column should be. Ted didn't need to read it; he knew exactly what I wanted.

For our next meeting, he dropped by a lunch appointment at an Indian restaurant, perfect as he was set to depart for India in a few days. He gave me a photo for the column which was still untitled. I cracked something about the Filipinos not having a derogatory term for foreigner and that the closest is "Hey, Joe." He liked it, having heard the term practically during his entire stay here in the Philippines.

Thus, on July 4, American Independence Day, of 1995, "Hey, Joe" made its debut in BusinessWorld.

It was one of four columns which I introduced to the section and the only one that still exists, in part because Ted is still here in the Philippines (the others had left) but mostly because people seem to like it very much, both the expat crowd and the Filipinos.

Ted has since written on many topics every week (save for the few times he was out of town and couldn't find a fax machine—or now a place to e-mail his column) from mundane stuff to social commentary and even a piece that featured Latin American-style magic realism. He has written about other countries too like India, Hong Kong, Thailand, Laos and, of course, the United States. But the ones I really like are the simple character sketches, chit-chats with ordinary folk from *balut* vendors to small-time entrepreneurs and, yes, the bar girls. Ted has a gift of observation and of turning these scenes eloquently and effortlessly into a simple tale of detailed ambience and atmosphere.

The insights he gets are oftentimes surprising and enlightening, and occasionally far-out, but always interesting.

Many of my favorite Ted Lerner articles are in this book. Most of them come from his columns but there are a few which are, should I say, commissioned articles. He told me that some of the articles here have been expanded since there are occasions when space constraints would limit his word count. So he went over them and wrote them the way he meant them to be.

There was a time when we almost lost Ted to another paper, which offered him space and more bucks. That's how it is in this business, although that's not our style. It would have been difficult to find a replacement for him. While there are others who could offer more serious, analytical social commentary, the column wouldn't be the same. "Hey, Joe" is more than just a foreigner's perception of life in the Philippines, but an adventure of one man who is fortunate enough to experience life's various facets and write about it. It's about one man who is brave enough to plunge himself with deliberateness into chaos because for him life is more interesting that way. Although he has been here in this country for quite some time, Ted is a backpacker at heart, still on the move to discover what's off the beaten track. So, I'm very grateful that he stayed with us.

Since last year, I'm no longer Ted's editor in BusinessWorld. I miss being the first one to read what he has to write about. What I don't miss is having to wait up for him to submit at the final hour, wondering where he's off to and if he would be able to submit at all and what would I put in his space. (He's reliable though, most of the time.)

Still, I take pride in being the one who recruited him for our team.

And I'm happy that finally Ted has a book. What more can the best man say?

So, Cheers! And hoping there's more on the way.

Vladimir S. Bunoan
Editor, Weekender Section
BusinessWorld

AUTHOR'S NOTE

The actual city of Manila is but one of fourteen cities and three municipalities that make up what is known as Metro Manila. Manileños usually just drop the "Metro" tag and call the entire metropolis Manila.

Metro Manila encompasses a land area of 646 square kilometers and is home to anywhere from eight million to 20 million people. The first figure is the official number. The second figure is the number which is more likely closer to the truth. Huge daily influxes from the provinces as well as many unrecorded births make an accurate count impossible. Either way, Metor Manila is one of the world's largest cities.

Also, the Philippine currency, the Peso, is herein represented simply by a capital "P" before the number. When some of the stories in this book were written, the peso traded at 26 to 1 against the US dollar. Then in July of 1997, economic crisis swept through Asia, turning many countries' currencies into funny money. The peso slipped to as low as 56 for 1 US dollar.

As of June 2007, the peso was trading at 46 to one dollar.

"These Filipinos are something, I'll tell ya," Eessel says. *"They have the most incredible way of smiling through hardship. They're born hustlers, from the time they're babies. Most of these people have nothing, yeh. Yet they're happy. Some of these people live in some of the most miserable conditions I've ever seen and when you meet them, they're happy and smiling. Filipinos are very clever at living."*

"My friend, for P50 your future will look very dark. But for P500 your future will look very bright."

--Bongeru, a local fortune teller

1

LIFE ON ARQUIZA STREET

From where I sit, on my second floor balcony, I can see it all. People of all shapes, sizes and fashions stroll by on the narrow lane below. On the sidewalk across the street, people gather around a fortune teller. At the *carinderia*(canteen) next door, the belly crowd gathers at the counter for their daily dose of beers, rum and a lot of idle conversation. Next door at the nondescript karaoke lounge, young Filipinas stand in the doorway and paint themselves up, preparing for the car loads of stressed out and moneyed up Japanese and Taiwanese, who will arrive later in the night. Boy the *balut* man strolls by and hollers his piercing pitch in to the early evening air.

This is Arquiza Street, a narrow three-block lane which runs parallel and near U. N. Avenue in the Ermita section of Manila. Here, in the middle block, between A. Mabini St. and M. H. del Pilar St., sits Tadel's Pension House, my home away from home.

Tadel's is the first place I ever stayed at when I first came to the Philippines. Before I actually lived in Manila, I basically resided at Tadel's for weeks at a time while in the country on extended stays. Even now I still sometimes visit Tadel's for a visit of several days, just for the fun of it.

Tadel's is a basic eight-room pension house. The place is owned by a Filipino couple, Elmer and Pilar. Actually, while the two are married, Pilar is the owner.

Elmer just works there. I never see either of them much these days. They both stay down in their home province of Masbate.

When I stayed at Tadel's, Pilar would only come around occasionally. She usually left Elmer in Manila to manage the place. Whenever I did see Pilar she would always relate some fantastical story to me. And always as if she were dead serious.

I recall one time I had come back to Tadel's after buying my morning coffee and newspaper when Pilar called me over.

"Psssssssst," she said waving me towards her.

"What's up," I asked. She had a serious look on her face.

"I just saw Ferdinand Marcos," she said flatly. "He's 34 years old now. He's alive again. He has seven lives. This is his second life. He's getting ready to distribute one million pesos to every Filipino." I checked to see if she was smiling. She wasn't.

"But if he distributes one million to every Filipino," I said, "then everybody will be just as poor." She wasn't listening.

"He plans to make business for everybody and every Filipino will have work. He has a 28-story condo in Makati right now. Just wait, you'll see."

"Does Imelda know about this?" I asked.

"No she's not involved this time around. Anyway I just came from Bicol. We've been digging for gold. We're about to hit it big. Next time you come here, this building will be ten stories instead of two." I suppose Pilar never did strike pay dirt. The only thing that's gone up at Tadel's over the last few years is the price.

My dealings with Elmer were usually much more down to earth. He's forever got a smile on his face. He's a born again Christian and loves to read the bible. He also loves to talk about any subject under the sun.

Whenever I was bored in my room, I could always find
a conversation in the small lobby with Elmer and his
various friends who stop by to talk story with him.

Elmer's tone of voice makes him sound like a Filipino
W. C. Fields. One very memorable quip of Elmer's came
late one night when I was asleep in my room at 2:30 in
the morning. I was abruptly awakened by a hideously
loud screeching sound. I ran to the balcony of my second floor room, looked down on the street below and
saw a man tearing up the street with a jackhammer.
Several onlookers just stood around smoking cigarettes,
as if nothing was happening. I ran downstairs and saw
Elmer standing on the front steps.

"Hey Elmer," I yelled above the extremely loud noise,
"why doesn't anyone say anything? It's 2:30 in the
freaking morning!!"

"Ahh yes, that is the number one problem with Filipinos," he said laughing, sounding like a Filipino W.
C. Fields. "They don't care!"

Besides the friendly, family-like atmosphere of
Tadel's, what really makes the place priceless are the
balconies in the rooms. All of Tadel's rooms are on the
second floor and the four facing the street come with
wide covered balconies. As a regular at Tadel's, they
always reserve me room number two.

From the second floor perch, I can peer out across the
rooftops of Ermita and see the area's skyline, including the Manila Diamond Hotel which juts into the sky
a kilometer away. More importantly I get a bird's eye
view of all the action, and non-action, going on up and
down the entire street below. This part of Arquiza St.
has it all, and is a rather cozy street. This block is really
a neighborhood in itself with many things happening,
all in a definitive laid back style.

Across the street I can see the different small businesses. Like every street in Ermita, there's a shop sell-

ing paintings, and, right next door, an antique shop. These shops never seem to do any business, a cold fact which does not seem to bother their owners, who rather seem to enjoy hanging out and chewing the fat.

On the sidewalk next to the antique shop a giant, ceramic pig stands smiling at all passers-by. This monstrous swine marks the entrance to the Hollandia bar, a small pub owned by a Dutchman named Ron. The Hollandia is always dead and way too quiet, except when the odd group of Germans or Dutchmen stop by to swill beer and talk loud.

Ron made the giant smiling ceramic pig. That's his real business. He exports these pigs and other people and animals made of ceramic to Europe and America, where their buyers place them on their manicured suburban front lawns for decoration. Inside on the floor behind the bar stands Ron's best seller, a small ceramic Elvis Presley. This Elvis has the face and hair of the young and dashing Elvis, but he's wearing the rhinestone studded white jumpsuit and cape of the older, doped-up Elvis.

Everyday outside the Hollandia, right next to the big pig, the friendly fortune teller from the southern Philippine city of Zamboanga sets up his office on the side walk. Bongeru shows up in the mornings and props up his hand painted sign advertising palm reading, astrological readings and faith healing. Several women also hang out with him, and I suppose they, too, tell fortunes. Bongeru never hurts for customers. There is always somebody who strolls by to avail of his powers. Bongeru works right on the sidewalk and this draws passers-by who like to listen in.

"In 1997," he told me once as several people stood nearby, "the Philippines will be visited by many catastrophes of nature. Including an earthquake sometime in February." Personally I tend not to believe seers, but

I always leave open the possibilities. Once when I was blowing smoke Bongeru's way, telling him how good he was, he quipped: "My friend, for P50 your future will look very dark. But for P500 your future will look very bright."

I know Bongeru is quite good at what he does. He once predicted to my wife that she had three moles on the back of her head which, even to my surprise, was true. Sometimes I stop by to see him before I go on a trip. I'll buy him a small pizza from the Shakey's Pizza across the street, or hand him a few pesos. Bongeru writes me a prayer on a piece of paper. He writes the prayer in Arabic and draws fancy designs on the paper.

"Always keep it with you on your trip my friend," he says, "It will protect you from all illness." And so far, it has not failed me.

The real action on Arquiza, especially at night, takes place a few doors away at the carinderia. Situated right in the middle of the block on the sidewalk, this place is the central meeting spot on Arquiza.

People come by to make phone calls, buy single cigarettes or small packets of shampoo, eat some *lugaw* (rice soup), play pool on one of the raggedy tables in the back, or sit at the dog-legged shaped counter and relax with a beer or a bottle of Tanduay rum. They generally hang out and talk a lot of nonsense.

This carinderia is owned by a man named Boy Lugaw. At least that's what the drunks there said his name was. Boy looks to be in his 40's. He's skinny but with a protruding round pot belly. He always wears loose fitting shorts, basic rubber slippers and a white sleeveless *sando* T-shirt which he wears pulled up and resting on top of his big belly. What's also funny about Boy is that sometimes you can see him come out from behind the counter, walk to the sidewalk, unzip his shorts, and urinate on his own building.

"Hey Boy," I always yell when I see him, "when's the baby due?"

"Three more months," he says with a laugh as he rubs his big belly.

I've noticed that many of Boy's customers also have big bellies. And like Boy, they all like to wear their shirts up and resting on their rotund stomachs. They sit around at the counter and drink beers and Tanduay rum until all hours of the night, watching all the passers-by and talking story. The belly crowd comes every night, except Sunday when the carinderia is closed, and every night they go deep into the well.

I have also noticed that many of these guys go by funny names like Boy's. Apparently there is an old tradition in the Philippines of people giving each other pen names as a way to identify people according to their most noticeable trait. Boy obviously makes a mean lugaw, although I have yet to sample it. Frankly I'm not that adventurous. But his name also differentiates him from Boy Balut, my favorite balut vendor who makes his rounds nightly. There's also someone they call Boy Under *de Saya*.

"What is the meaning of 'Under de Saya?'" I asked one of the belly crowd one night.

"Literally it means under the skirt," the guy said. "It means he always says yes to his wife."

"Anyway," said another guy with a pool stick in his hands. "His wife's a carabao." Everyone laughed. Boy Under de Saya shot back.

"Yes, but I found a new wife," he said.

Another character who hangs out at the carinderia is a skinny guy who goes by the name of Fernando Tanduay, as in the brand name of the rum. I've never been able to figure the reason for his constant presence there but every time I see him he always tries to work a deal.

"Hey boss, I wash your car," Fernando says. "Boss,

you come back, I want to show you something, very valuable. Where you stay boss? Parañaque? I've got a cousin out there who's selling a house. You like buy a house? I go with you there right now."

A big guy whom I always see hanging out at Boy's place is called Peping Matador. Apparently he's the house security as the drunks told me that someone named matador means he's an enforcer.

"Like they have in Tondo," said Boy Under de Saya. There's also this skinny old man, whose name I haven't caught yet, who is always offering up a roster of girls.

"Hey boss," he says in his whiny voice, "I got some good looking ones tonight. Here's my card, it's right around the corner. Ermita's not dead boss. Oh no, trust me. Best action in town."

Then there's a guy known simply as Sarge, as in sergeant. He works the door at the karaoke joint next door. Sarge never has much to say but he always gives me a friendly salute whenever I pass by. There's definitely something to be said about having one of the locals on the block salute you every time you walk down the street. Sarge is probably the most reliable guy on Arquiza St. You could trust a bag of money with Sarge and it'd be intact when you come back to get it.

Whenever I'm around on Arquiza St., everybody has a good laugh at my expense. One night Boy Lugaw tried to get me to eat his lugaw.

"What's lugaw anyway?" I asked him, knowing I was setting myself up for some jokes.

"Lugaw?" he said surprised. "This is lugaw." He showed me the big pot. "Rice porridge. It's got pig intestines, liver, skin, rice and boiled water. P10 per bowl. Come on Joe, you try." I realized lugaw contained all the unwanted scraps that were thrown out of the back of the meat house. My palate was not exactly moved by his description.

"Anything else in there?" I asked Boy. By now everyone was gathered around listening. I wondered what else could be in there. Perhaps the cousin of that dead rat laying on the street?

"Well," Boy said with a smile, "you don't see any dogs roaming around here, do you?" With that everyone broke down and laughed hysterically. I'll never know whether or not they were joking.

After I finished my beer I walked back across the street to Tadel's. Inside the lobby sat a Swiss man, whom I got to talking with.

"These guys were just telling me all about lugaw," I told him.

"Lugaw?" the Swiss man said. "What's this lugaw?"

"Well, as far as I could gather," I said, "lugaw is a mixture of all the unwanted scraps that they throw out the back. Come here I'll show you." We walked to the door and I pointed across the street to where the belly crowd was carrying on at Boy's place. "Look there. That's lugaw!"

HANGIN' IN MY NIPA HUT

I built a *nipa* hut. Well, I did not physically construct the thing. I had some guys do it for me. But it was my idea. And before my eyes it rose. Right in the middle of a subdivision in Metro Manila.

Actually, let's say it's half a nipa hut. The foundation is actually the cement roof of the car park. And the frame is made of coconut lumber, not bamboo. But the key element is there—the roof made of palm fronds. This distinguishes me from 99.999% of the people in my neighborhood and probably most other people in Metro Manila.

While the roof was being constructed, and for about a week after it was finished, the nipa hut caused a minor stir in my neighborhood. I noticed people walking by on the street below looking up and laughing and snickering to each other. The tricycle drivers who hang out at the bakery that sits diagonal from my house seemed to have derived some entertainment at my expense, as well. I haven't yet figured out why they would be laughing, but I suppose they never saw anyone building a nipa roof onto their house in Manila.

Probably it has something to do with status. People in the big city associate nipa roofs with province life. You build a nipa hut in the province when you're poor and do not have enough money to build with concrete, tile and tin sheeting. No matter that in the tropics, these products make for the equivalent of a Swedish

sauna bath. High falutin city folk just do not put up
leaves for their roofs.

Well, if they associate nipa with the poor provincial
life, that's up to them. I associate nipa with being cool.
Not cool as in hip. Like I said, nipa's hardly hip in the
city. I mean cool as in not hot. It's amazing how nipa
actually makes the most sweltering days pleasant
and tolerable. It's as if the nipa absorbs the heat and
cushions it, rather than radiating it like aluminum or
concrete.

Ever since my first trip to the Philippines, I have had
an affinity for nipa huts. That was in 1991 when I visited the island of Catanduanes in the Bicol region. I had
been directed there by a friend from Hawaii who was
a surfer. There's a wave that breaks in a remote spot
on the island and the locals there have set up several
surf camps along the beach to accommodate the foreign
surfers who trek there. I don't surf but went anyway
to enjoy hanging out.

I had no idea that June and July were the rainy
months and that foul weather was a possibility. I had
been soaking up the laid-back lifestyle of province life,
including the back-to-nature feel of my nipa hut. Then
one afternoon a typhoon began approaching. The sky
quickly started clouding up and turning nasty. When
the wind and rain started raging, I thought for sure
we were doomed. I especially thought this because all
I had for shelter was my flimsy nipa hut. Coming from
America, where people live in big solid houses, the nipa
hut seemed little match against nature's destructive
fury.

Several of us huddled inside my nipa hut and expected the horrifying winds to quickly blow this house
of twigs to smithereens. Amazingly, though, the nipa
hut came out unscathed. It swayed, it bent, but it didn't
break. It lasted the night. In the morning the worst had

passed and we were all safe.

I suddenly became impressed with the nipa hut and its clever design. A nipa hut is built to absorb the wind, thus cushioning the impact of nature's blustery wrath. That's why the nipa hut was moving from side to side but was not really in danger of being blown away. With a solid mass like concrete or tin, the wind slams up hard against the wall. That's why the wind can easily destroy a concrete wall. There's an adversarial relationship between the wall and the wind. This concept totally startled me. I started realizing for the first time that maybe these massive solid structures that I was used to in the west were not the only things that can adequately protect you against the elements.

It was also nice to realize that people can protect themselves from nature's anger and they don't have to go to the hardware store to do it. It is ingenuity born out of necessity, using whatever materials are available. Ever since that first trip to the Philippines, I've always loved nipa huts.

My nipa hut's sole purpose is not necessarily protection from the elements. Although we have used it for that reason in the three floods we had during the rainy season, thanks to the thoughtful Gatchalian real estate people, who build subdivisions without proper drainage. My nipa hut really serves as an escape from the oppressive heat of the house and as a sanctuary amidst the chaos of this city. All I have to do is climb the ladder to my nipa hut and I enter a new world.

Under nature's roof, I lounge in the hammock or the easy chair and look out the big open-air windows over the rooftops of the city. The big windows frame the outside world in a live, moving painting. One scene is framed by several coconut trees and offers ever changing skyscapes. Clouds drift by in the picture and then disappear, replaced by new formations and designs.

As the sun sets, the picture becomes a multi-colored bonanza. At night, hundreds of stars sparkle and shine on the black canvas.

Within this ever-changing painting come the airplanes. From where I sit I can see planes coming in for a landing and taking off at Ninoy Aquino International airport, three kilometers away. The landing planes come one after the next in a seemingly endless parade. My vantage point is such that I can see the planes lined up for arrival almost ten kilometers out into the sky. When they are seconds away from touchdown, I can actually read the name of the airline. But I'm not close enough to where I can hear the noise of the planes.

As the planes stream by, I sit and wonder about all the people who might be on board and the stories they could tell. *Balikbayans** returning home with hordes of cardboard boxes filled with canned goods from abroad, maybe coming back for a loved one's birthday or a funeral. Nervous foreigners who are visiting Manila for the first time and are looking to possibly invest money here. European couples coming on vacation. Diplomats flying in on an urgent mission. People up to no good.

When the planes leave, I wonder where the people are going and if they'll ever come back. I think about all the Filipinos on board, nervous and anxious as they leave the only land they have ever known for the unknown, just so they can help support the family back home. I think about the frightened Filipinas staring out at the fading city, as they head off to strange lands to marry men they have only known in letters.

When not looking at the passing scene, I listen. For some strange reason I can hear better in the nipa hut. Raised from the fray of Manila and up to the tree tops, I can concentrate on listening to the sounds of the

*A Filipino who lives overseas and returns home to visit the Philippines.

city, of which there are many. Manila pulsates with
sounds, especially at night. The sounds of dogs barking and fighting come from every direction. Once one
starts barking they all start up. The dummies just bark
and don't even know what they are barking at. Then
there's the constant hum of tricycles careening down
every street. The noise makes me realize that trikes are
everywhere and they breed like insects. In fact their
design—a motorcycle with a covered sidecar—makes
them look like giant cockroaches. I can also hear dishes
clanking, children screaming, hammers pounding,
horns blaring and roosters hollering.

In the nipa hut I can tune it all in or tune it all out.
My mind relaxes and drifts, and it's as if I am in a different world far, far removed from the tumult and fray
of Manila. In fact, the nipa hut is practically magical.
Not bad for something simple, cheap and definitely not
very trendy.

SUNDAY AT MANILA BAY

It is a typical Sunday along Manila Bay.

On the wall that overlooks the bay, and which stretches for nearly a mile, people sit and lounge. Occasionally couples, families or joggers pass by on the palm lined promenade. The traffic along Roxas Boulevard whizzes by, a sharp contrast to the usually jammed conditions any other day. On the ocean, cargo ships and oil tankers dot the near and far horizon.

The day is slightly overcast but there is a light breeze and the temperature is mild. Even the faint smell of sulfur blowing in off the ocean and the small stretch of beach strewn with garbage cannot dampen what is a pleasurable and relaxing afternoon.

"Hey Joe, you like a ride?" A *kalesa*—a horse drawn carriage—pulls up to the bench where I sit. The sign on the back of the carriage says "Black Beauty." "Two hundred pesos, one hour tour," the driver says. "Luneta, Rizal Park, Chinatown. I take you, Joe. Come, we drink beer."

"Naah, not today," I tell him.

"Then how about a nice beautiful Filipina," he says with a big smile as he moves his hands down over the invisible body of a voluptuous woman. "Then maybe you like come, yeh?" He cracks up laughing.

"Sure," I say, also laughing, "but certainly not with you. Anyway, how's business?"

"Oh, not bad," he says as he climbs down from the

carriage. "Up and down." He feeds his horse some grass, climbs back into the carriage and then trots on. "See you Joe."

Nearby where I sit, a mother lays asleep on a small patch of grass, her baby cuddled next to her. Children play in the ocean, diving for small crabs. The water is murky and looks filthy. I wonder how the kids can stand to swim in such dirty water. On the beach, which is littered with more garbage than I originally noticed, over twenty *banca* boats sit lined up. People mill around the boats, hanging out. Laundry hangs off several of the bancas. In one a man is sleeping. The boats have names like King Julius, King Hussein, Noel and 2 sisters, and 3 Brothers. The two guys sitting on the wall in front of me notice me looking at the boats.

"Hey, Joe!" says one and they both laugh. They both wear dirty T-shirts, loose shorts and worn out rubber slippers.

"Hey how ya doin'," I say. "How's the fishing today?"

"No we are not fishermen," says one. "These are ferry boats." Their names are Bert and Roy. They tell me they ferry passengers to and from the cargo ships and oil tankers anchored in the bay. P50 to the cargo ships, P100 to the oil tankers, which are anchored farther away.

I notice a sharp looking lady in high heels and a tight mini-dress standing on the beach waiting by the boats and I wonder why she is so well dressed. Then, just as I was about to ask Bert and Roy what she was doing there, a boatman picks her up in his arms and carries her to the banca sitting in the shallow water.

"She make short time boom-boom on the ship," Bert says, laughing a gap toothed grin. "It is illegal but they just pay the ship security guard and the customs man and—*walang problema!*"

A man and woman holding hands arrive and climb atop the wall. They jump down to the beach and fetch a boatman.

"That's a husband and wife," says Roy with the authority of experience. "He's a seaman. Been away many months. But his problem is too many children at home. Nowhere to go."

A soaking wet fisherman comes by carrying his spear and his catch—six long, skinny eels and a net full of small crabs. "Hey Joe, you like snake?" he asks happily. Everyone within earshot has a good chuckle.

I get up from the bench and take a seat on the wall. Coconut trees sway in the breeze for the entire length of the bay. A policeman cruises up and down on his motorcycle. Occasionally he stops to chat with the people hanging out. On a nearby bench a crowd of men sip gin and smoke cigarettes.

"Baluuuuut! Baluuuut!" A middle aged man with messy hair cruises by with his wicker basket full of magical, erotic eggs. Sitting on the wall, a girl named Sunshine asks: "Hey Joe, you like *balut*? Good for the knees. You make boom-boom." She laughs.

"Nope, sorry," I say, "I don't eat duck abortions." She laughs even harder. Five gruff looking foreign men walk by slowly, taking in the sights and sounds. They stop to chat. They say they are Albanian seamen.

"You eat balut?" Sunshine asks the one man who can speak a bit of English.

"What is this balut?" the man asks while his friends look on.

"Dead baby ducks inside an egg," I say. "They're supposed to make you strong at sex." He turns to his friends and explains the balut to them in their language. They all laugh loudly.

"Oh no thank you," the man says with a chuckle. "We have been at sea for two and one-half months. I do not think we need this, what do you call it?"

"Balut."

"Yes balut. Anyway it is difficult for us to enjoy Manila. We only make $200 a month. So we just walk around." They continue down the promenade.

On the footpath near where I sit, a man on a bicycle with a sidecar peddles in a circle. In the sidecar sit soft drinks and candy. A baby sits atop the bottles of Sprite. Then I hear the faint sound of a bell approaching.

"Ice cream, ice cream, ice cream. Five pesos only."

I buy Sunshine some ice cream. While we eat the sweet and cold treat, the sun, as if it had been waiting all day for this moment, peaks out from behind the clouds.

The sun is setting but the sunset will be hidden by the clouds. As evening approaches groups of women appear along the wall. They are all well dressed, made up and carry bags. The boatmen approach them and offer rides. A girl named Beauty—don't you just love girls' names in the Philippines—leans against the wall. She is out with her four year old niece to get some fresh air.

"They come out at night because they don't want to be seen," she says, a hint of disappointment in her voice. "Me? I don't want that kind of life."

Two policemen smoking cigarettes and drinking orange soda greet the waiting girls like old friends.

"When the girls come off the boat they pay the policeman," Beauty says. "In money or sex. One of the boats is owned by a policeman who's my friend." She says a Russian cargo ship has just today pulled into the bay. "It doesn't matter where the ships come from. The girls aren't choosy."

It is dark now, with the promenade illuminated by the soft glow of lamps that line the bay. Five ladies climb into a banca and the boatman starts the motor. Painted on the side it reads, "May God Bless Our Trip."

The boat sputters out into the darkened sea.
It is a typical Sunday along Manila Bay.

THE BOUNTY AMIDST
THE UGLY NIGHT

In the deepest part of the night, hours after sunset and hours before dawn, long after and long before another uproarious day, the ugliness of this city called Manila becomes magnified. The cloak of darkness, which should serve to hide this city's repulsiveness, its incredible amounts of garbage piled everywhere, its dirty old buildings sprawling in every direction, actually resonates the hard features. Slams them in your face. Forcing you to see this city up close and in more desperate and depraved detail.

One might assume that the quiet and cool of night would, if even for a moment, bring a respite from this hell. But it does not. During the day at least there is teeming life amidst all the ugliness. People are out and about moving, working, going places. Things are happening. And at least under the light of day you can stare at the occasional coconut tree that juts out of the concrete. Or you can look above the cement and steel sprawl at the sometimes brilliant blue sky and watch the clouds coming and going. Or you might even catch a sunset with the sky painted a multitude of brilliant colors. Nature still exists out there, even if you have to remember to look for it.

At night, though, there is nothing to distract your eyes from the lonely and festering piles of garbage that seem to grow bigger everyday and that nobody ever bothers to pick up. With the traffic and people no longer there, you can see just how much litter is strewn everywhere, not just on street corners. The dirty buildings, with their metal shutters in place, show themselves for what they really are—big, dark, filthy, ugly boxes lined up one after the next.

Cruise down EDSA, Manila's main thoroughfare, at four in the morning and you will see an ugliness like none other on earth. Dirty, cracked concrete, rickety building on top of rickety building. Everything man has built covered with layer upon layer of soot and filth. Electrical wires careening all over the place. The city at night is lonely and even more ugly than during the day. There can be little aesthetic beauty found in Manila anytime, especially at night.

Amidst the quiet depravity, however, life very much exists. Manila does not sleep. It merely slows down. It takes on a different rhythm, brought out by a different breed. The streets are less crowded but, in many ways, they are more wild. Decrepit trucks and buses that look like they could fall apart at any moment, many coming from the provinces, barrel across the pot holed concrete, going speeds their daytime counterparts can only dream of. They swerve from lane to lane belching thick plumes of black smoke, turning the dark night even darker.

Across the metropolis many people are out. Teenage boys spend the night hours washing taxis and jeepneys. People are hanging out at all-night canteens and 7-11s, smoking cigarettes, sucking balut, laughing, kicking back on cots on the sidewalk, resting in their trucks and taxis. It is the people that breathe life into this city.

And at the Balintawak market in Quezon City, the night positively comes alive. Here on EDSA, at the ramp leading to the North Luzon Tollway and the northern reaches of the Philippines, sits one of Manila's biggest and best *palengkes* (wet market). Balintawak is Manila's wholesale market, the first stop of all the vegetables and fruits which the farmers bring right out of the mountains of Northern Luzon, off the tollway and into the metropolis. This is where food sellers from all over Manila come to buy their daily stocks at prices half of any other market, load up their jeepneys and trucks and take the food back to their neighborhood to resell.

The Balintawak market is open 24 hours a day. The market really heats up, though, at around two in the morning because much of the food there has to be available to the hordes who will soon flood the city. Since anybody can buy there, I sometimes take to the deep night and venture to Balintawak to do some food shopping. Even though the lack of sleep often brings on drowsiness, Balintawak never fails to be exhilarating.

Standing at the top of EDSA, right at the turnoff to the North Expressway heading towards the Philippine summer capital of Baguio, I can see a bustling market stretching out for nearly a third of a kilometer. The place overflows with activity in the middle of the night. This is where Manila gears up for another day. People sell their wares from stalls under rows of strung up bare bulbs inside several large warehouse-like buildings. Other sellers spill out onto EDSA, taking up two lanes of the road, spread out a blanket and neatly arrange their fruits and vegetables in little piles. Buses stream by, slowing down just long enough for people to jump off. Everybody carries their colorful abaca and plastic *bayong* shopping bags, which will soon be filled with the bounty of the marketplace.

Exploring Balintawak is an assault on the senses. I start off with a bang in the meat section. My eyes are stunned by row after row of freshly killed pigs lying split open and spread-eagle on tables. My ears can hear

the chomp-chomp sound of shirtless men, cigarettes
dangling from their mouths, knife holsters strapped
to their waists, hacking at bone with their razor-sharp
bolos and slicing the dead pigs into pieces. It's an orgy
of bloody body parts everywhere, as if a horrific disaster
has recently befallen this place. Heads, all with the
same anguished expression, are piled on top of one
another. Intestines, giant livers, stomachs, and legs
hang from hooks.

The icing on the cake as far as the senses go is the
smell. The sense of smell tells you that what you are
seeing and what you are hearing is all very real. In
the meat section a harsh and rank smell of blood and
flesh fills the warm air. It is only a matter of moments
before I head for friendlier environs.

In the fish section, which runs down the sidewalk,
the bountiful catch of every kind of fish imaginable is
on display. Long skinny fish, big fat fish, little dried
fish, colorful fish are all piled on tables or inside tubs
of ice water. The water spills onto the ground making
walking a bit perilous. Ladies wearing long cotton
skirts, aprons, rubber boots and sleeveless shirts bark
out their sales pitches.

"Hey Joe, you like snake?" one smiling lady says to
me as she holds up a long eel. Several ladies standing
behind her also laugh. Around them people, many
carrying sacks of food, jostle for a space in the narrow
lanes and it is difficult to tell who is selling and who is
buying. Amidst all the sellers other people walk up and
down peddling everything from individual cigarettes,
rice cakes, hot coffee, pots and pans, plastic shopping
bags, fresh pancakes, towels and plastic stools.

I meander over to the friendliest and most colorful area: fruits and vegetables. The Philippines has
the most incredible amount of fruits and vegetables
I have ever seen. Different kinds of eggplant, shred-

ded bamboo, several varieties of potatoes, white and
purple onions, long *upos*, thick orange carrots, squash,
pumpkins, cabbage, tomatoes, yellow bananas, green
bananas, leaves of banana trees, trunks of banana
trees, piles and piles of ripe green watermelons, baskets
of *calamansi*(Philippine lemon), bright yellow mangoes,
green mangoes, bundles of white garlic, and other
spices and so many other things that I have never seen
before. The selection makes me realize how resourceful
Filipinos are. Everything has a use in the Philippines
and absolutely nothing goes to waste.

My bag now heavy with fresh food, and daybreak coming, I walk through the mass towards the car. I listen
to the sounds. Markets have such great sounds. People
haggling over prices, sellers barking, people shuffling
and running from place to place. It is the sound of life
at its core. There is nothing high tech here. It is just
people bringing the food to the people, who will then
bring it to the rest of the people. Balintawak is the
pulse of Manila.

As the night heads towards the dawn, the action of
the market mixes with the now waking city. The day's
first streak of light appears in the sky, the road becomes
more crowded and the city's first traffic jam appears.

Heading down EDSA towards home, I stare once
again at the awfulness around me. But the edge is not
quite there. For Balintawak has made me realize that
amidst the squalor and loneliness that a Manila night
highlights, there is life. There is bounty. And with it
Manila gets set to explode in its daily tumult.

ERMITA DREAMING

The day is gray and dreary with rain steadily falling. As usual, the traffic along M. H. del Pilar St. in Ermita is at a standstill. Noisy jeepneys fight with each other for every inch of space, ever so slowly creeping forward. On the sidewalks, people also jostle for position, their umbrellas touching as they go on their way.

"Dollar change mate?" says a security guard with a shotgun in his lap. He pushes open the door to the money changer inviting me in, but I walk past. I stop on the corner of del Pilar and Padre Faura, and stand under the canopy of the Japanese restaurant, waiting for the light to change. As I wait, I look down del Pilar at the horribly run-down and dilapidated buildings. I think about how this place used to be alive with action like no other place on earth. Now it looks like the kind of street your mother warned you never to walk down.

Suddenly, my vision turns hazy. Perhaps it is the rain blowing in my eyes. Or it could be that a slight fog has rolled in off Manila Bay. I continue to stare down the street, but all the shoddy old buildings are clouded over. A strange feeling has overcome me, as if I am dreaming. Then my vision clears and I can see lights on the buildings and they are no longer run down. Yes, it must be a dream because, in a matter of a few moments, del Pilar Street has suddenly, amazingly come alive.

This is most certainly a dream but I decide to run

with it. I cross the street to check it out. Ahh yes, the old Ermita, where every single base instinct of mankind is being played out right in the open. Wildly colorful neon lights flash from the buildings for several blocks on both sides of the street. On the corner a couple of midgets dressed in tuxedos holler at any passerby. They scurry around bow legged, grabbing people by the arm, trying to get them to come inside their bar. They grab me and open the door to their club, showing me about 30 bikini-clad girls dancing on the stage inside.

"No, no," I shout, laughing at the same time. I escape their clutches. All of a sudden, I have to sidestep a wheelchair coming the other way. The chair is occupied by an old white man who has a young Filipina on his lap. As I walk on, several girls from Bubbles disco across the street yell out for me.

"Hi there handsome," one shouts. "Come on over." I contemplate for a second but continue down the street, nearly stumbling over a guy lying on the sidewalk with stumps for legs and only one arm, the hand of which is out begging. I slip him a five peso note.

I walk into a place called Raymond's Fast Food, which is open to the street. Raymond's is run-down and drab in appearance. A lovely shade of faded lime green paint adorns the walls. Old wooden tables and chairs are lined up to the back of the room. But the appearance speaks nothing of the action here, which is quite lively this happy hour.

I pull up a stool at the sidewalk end of the long, oval-shaped bar and order a San Miguel. I consider this spot to be one of the best places in the world to watch people. I can watch the action inside and outside at the same time. It is three in the afternoon and the bar is filled with ugly and out-of-shape Australians and Europeans being hustled by Filipino girls. In the back of the room, Filipinos and foreigners play pool. On the scratchy jukebox, Rod Stewart is singing about the "slant eyed lady."

I barely have the first swig of beer down when a girl across the bar winks at me. She looks to be in her late twenties with about 50 years experience. Too much damn make-up. I smile back, though. Perhaps that was a mistake. Now she thinks I like her. My gaze upon this thing is interrupted by a tap on the shoulder. It is a guy selling imitation Oakley sunglasses.

"No, no," I say, "I'm not interested."

"I make you special deal," he says.

"No really, I don't want any." But he does not leave. He just stands there holding the glasses up for me to see. Behind him another guy stops and holds up a stack of knockoff cassette tapes. He butts in as the sunglass dude goes to bother someone else.

"You like tape?" he asks. I suck on my beer and look at the tapes. Madonna's Greatest Hits. The Best of Kenny Rogers. Sinatra and You.

"Not interested," I say. "But maybe if you had Zamfir, the master of the pan flute, I might think about it." He does not get it and goes away.

Now I see the girl who winked at me standing on the sidewalk. She's looking right at me with an "I'm-desperate-horny-I-like-you" kind of look.

"How ya doin' baby," I call to her. She walks over. "What are ya doin'?" Her make-up is so heavy it looks like a painted mask. She does not even bother to answer my question.

"I want you," she says shyly. "Take me back to your hotel."

"Nah. Not today," I say.

"Why not?" she cries softly. "I'll give you a massage."

"I'm just hanging out."

"Then give me P20."

"Why should I give you P20?"

"Because I'm hungry."

"Get outta here," I cry. "I bet you say that to all the guys." She sticks her tongue out at me and walks away. She stands on the sidewalk but looks back in to the bar. She winks at someone else and returns into the crowd, the "I'm-desperate-horny-I-like-you" look suddenly restored.

I order another P10 San Miguel. The guy to my left has been watching this and is laughing. Next to him on the bar are a dozen empty bottles of San Miguel and a paper plate with a half eaten piece of barbecued chicken.

"The money doesn't seem like much in the Philippines," he says with an accent that sounds German. "But it sure can add up."

"I bet it can," I say. It turns out he's Dutch. And he is in Manila getting all the things an ugly, overweight man in his fifties cannot get where he's from. At these prices, anyway. I ask him his name and he says "Eessel." But with his accent it sounds like he says "asshole." I tell him that and he just laughs. He's heard that one before.

"I've been coming to the Philippines for 15 years now," he says. "I love it here. I met my wife here. I met her when she was 14 here in Manila. When she turned 17, I married her and took her back to Holland. We stayed there five straight years. Now I've got some business here so we go back and forth."

"What's your business?" I ask.

"I've got some guest cottages down south. And I have an interest in a restaurant down the street." He introduces the big Filipino man next to him simply as his private security. Mr. Private Security is shifting from side to side, looking down the bar and out on the street. Evidently, he's trying to find someone.

"Where's that nigger!" he says in broken English. "I beat the shit from him." He's obviously on the war path and I make sure to be as friendly as possible.

"What's his deal?" I ask Eessel.

"Oh, he's looking for that black guy that's been walking in and out of here. The guy's been trying to pick up my lady over here." I look and see a gorgeous young girl standing behind Eessel. Early twenties, smooth dark skin, long shiny black hair.

"Is that your wife?" I ask.

"No," Eessel says. "I'm trying to get this one to go 'short time' with me."

"Where's your wife at," I ask.

"Oh, she's back at the hotel."

"So, where do you go?"

"I know a great short-time hotel down the street here. P100 for three hours."

My view of Eessel is suddenly obstructed. The man with the cassettes is back. He just stands there with a grin on his face and the tapes in the air. I shoo him away. Eessel reaches for his chicken when he's distracted by a tug at his pants. Two grimy street urchins, perhaps four years old and wearing only filthy white sleeveless T-shirts and no pants or underwear, eye the half eaten piece of chicken and hold out their hands. Eessel hands it over. The two bare-ass little boys scamper down the street as excited as if they had just found a pot of gold at the end of the rainbow.

"These Filipinos are something, I'll tell ya," Eessel says. "They have the most incredible way of smiling through hardship. They're born hustlers, from the time they're babies. Most of these people have nothing, yeh. Yet they're happy. Some of these people live in some of the most miserable conditions I've ever seen and when you meet them, they're happy and smiling. Filipinos are very clever at living."

"So, what's with the security," I ask him.

"Doing business in the Philippines is a risky thing. I knew a couple of guys who had a farm down south in Mindanao. One day, a bunch of guys with guns came and knocked on the front door and said, 'You have three hours to get out. This place is ours.'"

"And did they leave?"

"Sure they did. It was either that or be killed. The next day the thugs were running the business." Eessel turns around and says something to the girl. "Nice meeting you, Ted. I'm going short time with this one here." He shakes my hand and walks out of the bar and into the street, holding hands with his new girl friend, both following Mr. Private Security.

I turn my attention back to the bar. The place is filled with people buying and selling each other. At one table several worn-out looking women sit playing with their babies. Out on the street, an endless stream of jeepneys drive by spewing their diesel fumes into the air. Some guy then tries to sell me sour mangoes. Another guy comes right on his heels and offers steamed corn on the cob.

I get up from the stool and walk outside on to the sidewalk. The rain falls steadily on my head. Before I walk down the street, I turn around to have one more look at Raymond's. But the place, as I had just known it, is no longer there.

When I come to, I am standing outside what used to be Raymond's Fast Food. Now the building, like nearly everything else in this once incredibly lively, small stretch of Ermita, is boarded up, dilapidated, and dead.

My dream having given way to reality, I continue walking slowly down the nearly empty sidewalk. On the street jeepneys still jostle for a space. A light mist continues to fall and my mind lingers. I think about

how those who are always concerned with image, never
with the reality of survival, could never appreciate a
place like Raymond's, in an area like Ermita. To these
kinds of folks, Ermita in the 1970's, 80's and early 90's,
as a red light district which catered mostly to foreigners, was considered a black mark. Now as a run down
hell hole, well, nobody ever says much of anything
about it.

But anyone with even an iota of empathy for his fellow man understood what a fascinating, downright
entertaining place Ermita used to be. It was full of that
bare knuckle, no holds barred, real-life honesty that
one cannot easily find in too many places on earth. On
top of this, Ermita had an almost indescribable charm.
In its day Ermita indeed had it all. And for those who
remember it the way it was, they know that that was
no dream.

"That's the understatement of the year," Matt said. "They have a room next to the bar called 'The Office.' That's where they conduct business, if you know what I mean. When I went to this place, there was no sign, no lights out front, and no electricity. To get in you have to knock on this big metal door. A slot opens and a pair of eyes look at you. If they see you're all right, then they'll let you in. When we walked in there was nobody there and the place was dark. But all of a sudden, a bartender comes out of nowhere with a cold San Mig, the piano player turns up and sits at the old piano, they light a few candles and put them on the piano and the girls come over from the dorm across the street. You could be the only one there and, no matter the time of day, they'll open it for you."

CAN'T BUY MY LOVE

Hospitality and loyalty are two traits Filipinos are legendary for. And in Thailand these days, the word about that has no doubt spread very fast.

It was late September, 1995, when a group of 15 Thais arrived in Manila for the World Boxing Federation mini-flyweight championship of the world, a fight which was to take place five days later. Among the group were several boxers, including the champion Fhasang Pongsawang, his manager, Songphol Pongsawang—a former Bangkok police lieutenant, now a wealthy night-club owner and boxing promoter—several other boxers and the trainer. The remainder of the group consisted of newspaper, radio and television journalists.

There to meet them at the airport were the promoters of the fight, Johnny and Liza Elorde, of the legendary Elorde boxing family, along with several of their assistants, including Dodong, who was to escort the Thais throughout their stay in Manila.

The World Boxing Federation is not one of the top organizations in professional boxing, but its mini-fly-weight title that was up for grabs that year in Manila had been generating a lot of interest in the Philippines and Thailand. The hometown boy, Ronnie Magramo, all of five feet tall, would be trying to win back the title he lost to Pongsawang in July in Bangkok, on a controversial unanimous decision. In that fight Magramo was the aggressor all night, chasing his Thai opponent around the ring for 12 rounds. But, for some reason, the judges, all foreign, gave the decision, and the title, to the Thai.

Luckily for Magramo his managers, the Elordes, had stipulated in the contract for that first fight that should Magramo lose the title, a rematch would take place in Manila. Thus, "The Great Rematch" was born.

After some ceremonial picture taking at the arrival area of the airport, the entire Thai group was handed over to Dodong and a driver, who would take them to the Grand Boulevard Hotel on Roxas Boulevard. Most of the Thais, including the manager, Songphol, could not speak English so one of the Thai journalists acted as interpreter. Regardless of the language barrier, though, they were impressed with the hospitality from the start.

The Thais were given a police escort, hired by the Elordes, all the way to the hotel. The fight contract allowed for three free rooms, along with food and transportation for five people, the standard in professional boxing. The Thais, however, needed more rooms. While Liza Elorde made clear she could not pay for the extra guests, she was able to get the Thais a 40% discount on three extra rooms. While the group was checking in, Liza even gave them tips on how to pile extra people in to the room without the hotel noticing. The Elordes then gave their suite at the hotel to Dodong, just so he could be available to the Thais 24 hours a day. They made available a 15 seat van with a driver to take the Thais wherever they wanted to go, and do whatever they wanted to do.

The hospitality showered upon the Thais was a marked contrast to how the Filipinos were treated when they went to Bangkok back in July for the first match. The expenses for five people were paid, but after that there was not much else. They had a driver who

picked them up upon arrival in Bangkok, took them to
the weigh-in the day before the fight and to the arena
the day of the fight. But if Johnny and Liza Elorde
wanted to go out to a restaurant, shopping or simply
tour the sights of Bangkok, they were on their own.

In addition, Thai manager and promoter, Songphol
Pongsawang, paid Magramo's $45,000 purse in Thai
baht, instead of dollars as the contract specifically
stated. Stuck with a sack full of over 1 million baht, the
Elordes were forced to have the fight's matchmaker,
a Thai, go out in the middle of the night in Bangkok
to find somebody to change the baht into dollars. He
came back with the dollars, but not before a restless
night for the Elordes.

On top of this, during the weigh-in the day before
the fight, the Thais would not allow the Elorde camp
to test the weighing scale for accuracy. Consequently
Ronnie Magramo weighed in overweight and was
forced to workout on the spot in order to lose the extra
weight. When fight time arrived, the Thai announcer
introduced Magramo first, when as champion he should
have had the honor of being introduced last. After the
fight the Elorde camp was not even offered a ride back
to their hotel. They had to ask. And even though they
felt they were robbed of a decision, and their title, the
Elordes left Bangkok quietly the next day.

Filipino hospitality being what it is, however, things
would be different in Manila. A musician by trade,
Dodong had even cancelled a six month contract to
play in Japan just so he could help out his friends, the
Elordes. And he went about his job of escorting the
Thais in classic Filipino fashion; he catered to their ev-
ery whim, treating the Thais as if they were old friends.
He drove them around Rizal Park and showed them
the important monuments and buildings of Manila.
He took them to the cockfights at the Elorde Sports

Complex in Parañaque. He brought them shopping at Pistang Pilipino in Ermita and SM department store in Makati, where the manager, Songphol, bought Dodong a new coat. He also took the Thai entourage, now with several new arrivals numbering nearly 20, to the Thai embassy in Forbes Park, where they waited for three hours before they met the Prime Minister of Thailand, who was in Manila on an official visit.

When they went out to eat, Dodong sometimes would taste the food first, just to show the Thais that he was looking out for their best interest. One time when one of the Thai reporters needed to urgently send film back to his newspaper in Bangkok, Dodong drove the reporter to the airport and took him to the Thai Airways office. There the reporter was able to phone the pilot in a plane just about to leave for Bangkok. Heeding the reporter's plea, the pilot agreed to take the film to Bangkok personally.

On their second night in Manila the manager, Songphol, asked Dodong to set him up with some girls.

Said Dodong, "I said to him politely, 'I'm sorry sir. I am not a meat dealer.' I didn't take them to a girlie bar. I didn't want to be responsible if something bad happened." Instead Dodong took 16 of them to the Lost Horizon disco in the five star Westin Philippine Plaza hotel. "I think they were disappointed. The manager was cranky all week because he couldn't get a woman."

The lack of women notwithstanding, Dodong's warmth and hospitality had won him new friends. "They trusted me so much," Dodong said. "The manager said if I ever come to Bangkok, he'd return the favor." And the feeling was mutual. "I liked the Thais. I liked the boxer, Fhasang, very much. He couldn't speak English, but I could see it in his face. He was a very nice guy."

On the night of the fight, Saturday, Sept. 30, Typhoon

Maneng was rampaging through Manila. Still, over three thousand people turned out at Ninoy Aquino Stadium to see little Ronnie Magramo try to win back his title from Fhasang Pongsawang. They were glad they came. After an exciting undercard—the exception being a dud heavyweight contest featuring two Canadian ex-commercial fishermen, which lasted only 59 seconds—the title match proved to be the fight of the year in the Philippines. Instead of running as in the first fight, Pongsawang chose to fight. Pongsawang hit the canvas once in the early rounds, but slowly came back in the middle of the fight and looked to be in control. Magramo, however, showing the courage that Filipino fight fans love, went wild in the tenth round, flooring Pongsawang with eight straight right hands and knocking him out. The WBF mini-flyweight title was back in the Philippines, and this time Ronnie Magramo made sure there was no controversy.

The action at the arena that night, however, was not confined to the ring. As is the custom at boxing matches in the Philippines, there was a lot of gambling taking place amongst the crowd. And Songphol Pongsawang was right in the middle of it. He, along with several other Thais in the audience, had bet around 100,000 baht on their fighter, which is equivalent to the same amount in pesos. When it came time to pay up, however, the Thais paid in baht. The bet takers in Manila work in pesos or dollars only and they could be heard wondering what they were going to do with all the useless Thai baht. They only calmed down when an executive from Union Bank, who just happened to be in the crowd that night, said he would exchange the baht at his bank on Monday.

In addition to this impropriety, throughout the night the Thais were dictating the promotion to Liza and Johnny Elorde even though it was the Elordes who

were putting on the event. As previously agreed, the
Thai manager had purchased satellite time and was
showing the title fight live back to Bangkok. But, going against the terms in the contract, he instructed his
people to put placards on the ring apron advertising an
energy drink called M1-50. Liza Elorde pointed out that
Songphol was paid $40,000 by M1-50 in Thailand and
didn't offer any to the Elordes. And the Thais refused
to take the placards down.

The Thais then demanded telephone hotlines to
Bangkok. Then they started videotaping the undercard,
which they hadn't paid for. Liza Elorde immediately
approached Panya, a Thai journalist who was the interpreter, and demanded $5,000 for the rights to show
the undercard. They bargained down to $2,000. But as
soon as the agreement was reached, the Thais stopped
taping the undercard. They then approached Johnny
Elorde and agreed on $800 to tape only the heavyweight
contest. On top of all this, just before the title match,
the Thai manager stalled his fighter's entrance to the
ring by 25 minutes because he was waiting for the clock
to reach 10:30 so the fight could go live to Thailand.

While all this was going on, Dodong stood in the
corner of Pongsawang. Caught in a bit of a quandary
as to who to root for, he chose not to cheer for either
fighter. But the Thai manager, now placing utmost
trust in Dodong, gave his Filipino escort 16,000 baht
to hold and wager on his behalf.

But what really seemed to cement their relationship,
as far as the Thais were concerned, was what Dodong
did after the fight. One of the Thai fighters needed
stitches for a cut over his eye. Dodong, with a police
escort hired by the Elordes, accompanied the boxer, and
the Thai entourage, to the Ospital Ng Manila. When it
was discovered that the hospital had run out of stitch-
ing, Dodong and the policeman drove to Philippine

General Hospital in a torrential rain to get stitches. Back at the Ospital Ng Manila, the doctor had just begun sewing the cut when the power went out.

Dodong then went and got a flashlight from the van, and held it up while the doctor repaired the wound. Recalled Dodong: "The Thais told me, 'Dodong you have a very nice heart. You are a good man.'"

There was, however, this matter of the uncollected $800. Dodong had been instructed by Liza Elorde to collect the money from the Thais. The $800, however, went unpaid that night. Dodong had told Liza at the arena that he had asked the Thais after the fight to pay the money, but that they refused, and would pay later. The Thais were scheduled to leave for Bangkok Sunday evening, the next night. Dodong figured he still had some time to collect from his new friends. But he didn't realize that the Thais had other ideas, ones that would nearly cause an international incident.

***

Sunday, Oct. 1 dawned cloudy and damp, but at least the worst from Typhoon Maneng was over. After a hectic night of putting the finishing touches on their boxing promotion, and celebrating Ronnie Magramo's heart-stopping victory over Fhasang Pongsawang, Liza and Johnny Elorde managed to get a few hours sleep. They rose early in the morning and, as they do every Sunday, went to church with their family in Parañaque. Their work, however, was not quite yet finished. The fight would be aired over Channel 13 that night, and, after church, Liza would have to spend the day finalizing the list of sponsors whose commercials would air during the telecast.

There was also the money the Thais owed to the Elordes, but, frankly, Liza was not that worried about collecting. The amount they owed now totaled

$1,134—$800 for the rights to videotape the heavyweight contest, $254 for two additional rooms on top
of the three extra rooms the Thais rented at the Grand
Boulevard Hotel, and $80 for the license issued by the
Games and Amusements Board. When the Elordes
were in Bangkok for the first match, they paid all their
bills. They couldn't imagine the Thais doing otherwise
in Manila. Besides the Thais weren't scheduled to fly
back to Bangkok until 10 o'clock that night. And Liza
trusted Dodong and figured he would not have a problem getting the Thais to pay.

By Sunday morning, however, Dodong still had not
collected anything. Over breakfast at the Grand Boulevard Hotel coffee shop, Dodong had asked Panya,
the interpreter, for the money. Panya had said, "Don't
worry Dodong, we will pay you the money." Panya did
not say when, though. And Dodong, not wishing to
appear rude to his guests, did not push the issue. It
was after breakfast, however, that Dodong got his first
inkling that he might have a problem on his hands.
Dodong had promised to take the Thai entourage to
the Pistang Pilipino shopping complex to do some last
minute shopping. As the group gathered in the lobby
of the hotel preparing to leave, the Thai manager,
Songphol, and Panya, his interpreter, went to the
front desk to settle the bill. Dodong noticed that the
Thais and the front desk clerk seemed to be having a
bit of an argument. After the Thais left the front desk,
Dodong approached the clerk and asked, "Excuse me
sir, is there any problem?"

"Yes," said the clerk. "They refused to pay P61,000 (~
$2,300) that they owe. Who will pay us the balance?"
When Dodong heard the amount he was stunned.

"P61,000? Don't worry," he reassured the clerk,
"the hotel will get the money. I'm with the Elordes.
Everything's guaranteed." The clerk nodded and said

he understood.

Dodong, not sure what to make of this latest turn of events, immediately called the office at the Elorde Sports center in Parañaque. Liza and Johnny, however, were still at church. Dodong told Liza's secretary, Imelda, that the Thais would pay the $1,134 at the airport. Not wanting to get anyone worried, and still not sure what he should do, he did not even mention the P61,000 to Imelda.

Dodong then took the Thais to Pistang Pilipino for some shopping. At around noon they came back to the Grand Boulevard. As soon as they arrived at the hotel, the Thais asked the desk to retrieve their luggage and bring it downstairs. The Thai manager, Songphol, then asked Dodong to take them to lunch.

Five Thais, including the manager and Panya, then went down the street to the Aristocrat restaurant, accompanied by Dodong. As they ate their chicken barbecue and java rice, Songphol turned to Dodong and, speaking through Panya said, "Dodong is your passport with you today?"

"No," Dodong replied. "My passport is in my house."

"Dodong," Songphol continued, "I want you to fly with me to Bangkok tonight, if you have your passport." Dodong was impressed. Perhaps, he thought, since I have been so good to the Thais over this past week, Songphol wants to do this for me in return.

Moments later Songphol, again speaking through Panya, turned to Dodong and said, "Dodong, we are going to pay you the money, but it's only for you. If you are going to pay Johnny and Liza, we're not going to pay you the money."

"Yes, no problem," was all Dodong could think to say. Showing them how much he needed the money, he even pulled out his wallet to show the Thais that it was completely empty. Then he showed them that he had only four pesos in coins in his pocket. But deep inside, Dodong was beginning to doubt the Thais.

At 3:30 pm Liza Elorde was back in her office at the Elorde Sports Center, when she received a call. It was Dodong.

"Dodong, where are you now?" she asked.

"I'm at the hotel," he replied.

"Dodong, did you get the $1,134?" She still didn't know about the P61,000 hotel bill. Dodong was not about to tell her.

"No, the Thais don't want to pay." Liza was getting anxious.

"Dodong, don't let them leave the hotel unless they pay me."

"They refuse to pay," Dodong said. "Here talk to Panya." Dodong handed the phone over to Panya, who had been standing nearby.

"Panya, where are you now?" Liza asked him.

"We're out shopping," he answered.

"You better pay me the $1,134," she said with a hint of anger.

"We'll pay the $334," Panya said. "But not the $800. The heavyweight fight only lasted 59 seconds."

"But Panya, we had an agreement!" Panya laughed as if it was no big deal.

"I'm serious," Liza shot back. "You will pay us. I'll call hotel security."

"Don't worry," Panya told her. "Dodong is with me. I'll give Dodong the money." He then passed the phone back to Dodong.

"Dodong, Panya said you were shopping. Where are you now?"

"We're still in the hotel," Dodong said. "They already checked out. They're loading the van now. They want to go to the airport right now."

"But Dodong, it's only four o'clock. Their flight doesn't

leave until 10."

"But they want to go now."

"Dodong, just stay there at the hotel. Don't let the Thais leave. I'll call security."

"Ok," Dodong said reassuredly, "I'll stay right here."

Liza immediately called security at the Grand Boulevard hotel.

"The Thai guys are in the lobby," she told the security officer anxiously. "Please hold them because they owe us a thousand dollars."

"No problem Mrs. Elorde," the security man said. "We'll go right to the lobby."

"We're going to the hotel," Liza told him. "Hold them, we'll be right there."

One minute later Liza received a call from the security man at the Grand Boulevard hotel.

"Mrs. Elorde we can't find the Thais in the lobby. The doorman said they just left. In a van and another taxi."

"They left?!" Liza shouted. "With our van and a taxi?"

"Yes ma'am." Liza then called the front desk of the hotel thinking that the Thais might still be around.

"Are you Mrs. Elorde?" asked the front desk clerk.

"Yes."

"Mrs. Elorde, the Thais didn't pay for the additional three rooms. They insisted it be charged to you. It comes to P61,000."

"P61,000! I won't pay for that. You should have charged the Thais."

"Ok, Ok," the clerk said. "Where can we get in touch with them?"

"They just left for the airport," Liza said. The clerk put down the phone and Liza could hear him telling someone to quickly get hotel security to the airport.

Then he picked up the receiver again. "Mrs. Elorde, our security is on the way to the airport. And we're alerting our people at our reservations desk there to be on the lookout. Why don't you meet us at the airport?"

"Alright," Liza said, "we'll meet you at the departure area." As she put the phone down, Liza was beside herself. "Where's Dodong's loyalty?" she yelled. "Why did he leave the hotel?"

In a panic Liza took out her phone book and looked up the numbers of some friends, all the while cursing Dodong. She would deal with him later, though. Now it was time to ask for a few favors. First she called up some people she knew at Immigration. When she told them that the Thais owed her $3,400, and were on their way to the airport to try to escape the country, the Immigration people immediately brightened up. Apparently they liked this kind of action.

"We'd be happy to do the job Mrs. Elorde," the man from Immigration told her. "Maybe they're upset because they lost last night. Just come to the airport. We'll hold them if they try to leave."

Liza then called a friend of hers from the traffic enforcement group that works the departure area at the airport. He, too, said his people would be delighted to help and they'd be on the lookout for the Thais. Johnny, who had come over from the cockfights next door, now joined Liza in the office and made a call to the Parañaque police. He requested a police escort to the airport. The police happily obliged and immediately sent a man to the Sports Center.

The Thais were now facing a veritable armada of Philippine officialdom in their attempt to flee the country. It was only several minutes before the policeman arrived at the Sports Center. Johnny would go to the airport while Liza would stay behind to monitor any new developments. But as Johnny headed for the

door, with the policeman trailing behind, he suddenly
stopped in his tracks. Liza who had just picked up the
phone, dropped the receiver on the table. They were
dumbfounded at what they saw standing at the office
door. It was Dodong.

"Dodong, where are the Thai people?!!" Liza yelled.

"Don't worry," Dodong said. "They're here with me."

Stuck in the middle, between his friends Johnny and
Liza Elorde, and his guests, the Thais, Dodong chose the
loyalty of friendship, and also of country. After his last
conversation with Liza, when she told him to keep the
Thais at the hotel, Dodong realized he had to act on his
own and act fast. Any attempt to collect from the Thais
at the hotel or at the airport would, he figured, become
a public mess involving too many people. His only choice
was to fool the Thais into thinking they had him on their
side. After putting the phone down he turned to the 20
Thais waiting anxiously in the lobby.

"Ok, we'll leave now," he said. "Come hurry, we'll
go straight to the airport." The Thais were ecstatic.
Dodong called the driver, who brought the van over.
Speaking in Tagalog, Dodong gave him instructions on
what to do. Then he flagged down a Tamaraw FX taxi.
He instructed the bell boys to load all of the Thais' luggage in the taxi, in which he would ride. He then asked
who was holding all the airplane tickets, and told that
person to ride in the taxi too. The manager, Songphol,
and Panya rode in the van.

With the taxi leading the way, and Dodong inside
along with all the luggage and the tickets, the entourage left the Grand Boulevard hotel for the airport. Or
so the Thais thought. When they took a left turn on
to Quirino Ave., instead of going straight down Roxas
Blvd. in the normal route to the airport, one of the Thais
asked, "Dodong, is this the way to the airport?"

"Yes this is the way," Dodong told him. "It's a short

cut. With all the rain it may be flooded the other way. Anyway, before you leave, since it's still early, I'll show you around Manila. We have a very interesting road, the South Super Highway. You must see it. And a cemetery, Manila Memorial Park. Like nothing you've ever seen." The Thais had no idea the South Super Highway led right to the Elorde Sports Center in Parañaque and that Manila Memorial was right across the street.

Along the way the Thais kept asking, "Dodong why is it taking so long?" Dodong was able to calm their worries when, while driving through the Magallanes area, a plane flew directly overhead.

"See," Dodong said with a smile. "There's the airport."

When they finally turned into the parking lot of the Elorde Sport Center, one of the Thais turned to Dodong and said, "Dodong, are you looking for trouble?"

"No, no," Dodong said. "I do not think it is me who is looking for trouble. We are here to say good-bye to Johnny and Liza."

"No don't do that," the Thai said with a hint of panic in his voice. "No more good-byes."

The taxi pulled up and parked at the front door. The van parked right behind. Speaking Tagalog Dodong gave instructions to the driver to stay put. Dodong then got out of the cab and told security not to let anyone leave. He then went inside to the office. The Thais stayed where they were. The masses from the cockfight, curious at these foreign guests, peered at the Thais from the balcony. The Thais were not too ecstatic anymore.

After several minutes Panya went inside to the office and faced the Elordes, Dodong, their staff and a policeman.

"What's the problem?," he said casually, trying to act innocent.

"You owe us money!" Liza shot back. She was not in the mood for a friendly chat. "And what about your hotel bills Panya?"

"I don't know anything about any hotel bills," he said. "We can't pay you the $800. The heavyweight fight lasted only 59 seconds."

"You're giving us headaches," Liza yelled. "I've had enough of this. You owe us $3,420 all in all. Go outside and ask your manager for the money. If you don't pay me, you cannot leave the Philippines. I already called Immigration."

Panya could see Liza was not joking. He went outside to see his manager, who was still sitting in the van. Several minutes later he came back to the office.

"Here's your money," he said, handing the dollars to Liza. She counted it. Thirty $100 bills.

"Oh no," Liza said. "You're still $420 short."

"Lets bargain," Panya said.

"I'll tell you what, we'll bargain for $20. I want $400 more."

"I think $3,000 is enough," Panya said.

"Here's your $3,000 back!" Liza shouted, handing him the money. "You complete this, or you cannot leave the Philippines. You're not in Thailand anymore. You're in the Philippines. You'll all go to jail. Go back to your manager and get the money."

Panya left the room. He came back several minutes later and threw the money on the table. Liza counted it. $3,400.

"Is everything Ok?" Panya asked.

"It's fine," Liza said. "Don't do that again. You can never come back to the Philippines if that's your attitude." Even though she planned to call Immigration and tell them the problem was solved, she told Panya, "If you encounter problems at the airport, it's not my business anymore."

As the entourage made its way to the airport, several Thais were angry with Dodong. He tried to explain his position.

"My friend, I am responsible if this is not settled. I am in the middle. You must understand." With that they seemed to calm down. Once at the airport, the group was met by the Grand Boulevard security. Dodong told them everything was settled. As the bags were being unloaded, Dodong shook hands with several of the Thai journalists. The manager, Songphol, and Panya stood off to the side, saying nothing and making sure their eyes did not meet Dodong's. As the group started to move towards the terminal, Dodong waited for them to approach him. They never did. Apparently ashamed, they left Manila without a hand shake, a thank you or a good-bye.

Late that night at the Pizza Villa restaurant in the BF Homes subdivision near the Elorde Sports Center, at a small party held to celebrate Ronnie Magramo's victory, Dodong was the center of everyone's attention. Being modest, but obviously enjoying the moment, he joked, "It was not heroism, it was capitalism. Johnny Elorde's like a brother to me. If I take the money and go to Bangkok, I can never come back to the Philippines again. As they say, you can't buy my love."

Certainly the Thais, at the time on their way to Bangkok, would not argue with that.

FILLING IN THE GAPS

One of the more interesting and intriguing facets of living in a country where the majority of the people are poor, is finding out just how people manage to survive on a day to day basis. In any of the so-called Third World countries which I've visited, and here in the Philippines, I've always noticed the amazingly creative things people do in order to put a little rice and fish in their bellies.

For instance, there is a whole genre of people in Manila who have created work for themselves where none technically exists. You might call them gap fillers. Like flowing water that naturally finds its own way, seeping in wherever there are cracks, they fill gaps that society leaves open and make something out of it for themselves.

In essence, many are brokers, or middlemen. Sometimes they perform a much needed service. If you run into an honest one, they can bring you tremendous slack. They can prevent you from having to worry about where you are going to leave your car. They will carry your bags and save you from ruining your back. They can instantly satisfy a voracious hunger. They can find things you otherwise might never find.

Of course, since this level of society works without any specific rule book, there's always that chance of getting fleeced. Good or bad, though, these people fill a need, or simply make one up. They are people who have created a job for themselves, put themselves into position to get in the middle of some transaction, in hopes of lifting some of the cash from whatever deal is about to go down. And they are an essential part of the economic life of the city and country.

Gap fillers and brokers seem to thrive wherever there are people or goods being moved from one place to the next. A perfect example is the people you meet every time you stop somewhere to park your car. At a glance, it's fairly obvious that these people, whom you can find in public places like the Luneta park, outside the immigration office, certain shopping malls and nearly every street outside of the business district of Makati, have gotten the job of car watcher merely by appointing themselves to it. Over a period of time, they must have staked out the area, divided it up among the others who also hang around there, and have put themselves in position, creating a job where none previously existed.

As you drive up looking for a place to park, they always appear out of nowhere and flag you down, waving you into a space. Often times, you'll see kids rush up to you first. But in the parking business, seniority and a healthy respect for your elders obviously counts, as it is the elders who always saunter over, brush the kids aside and take charge.

The more entrepreneurial of them will open the door for you and ask if you want the car washed. Either way, watching your car is a given, really, as it is their territory, so that part does not even need to be brought up. And generally, I've found that with these people, you can even feel that your car, its tires, and all the contents inside will be there when you get back. And even if you come back two days later, the same person who waved you in will magically appear out of nowhere, popping out of the bushes from an afternoon siesta as soon as you are about 10 meters from your car.

"Good afternoon, sir," they say with a smile as they hustle over to your car. Even if cars can't be seen coming for three kilometers in every direction, they'll still back you out of your spot with some quick tapping on the back end of the car, a few waves, perhaps a whistle and then a well placed hand laid out in your direction where you, of course, fork over the appropriate amount of paper notes and/or coins.

Another place to run into gap fillers is at bus terminals, although the people who work and hustle the bus terminals can be a little harder to figure out than the parking people. The hustlers at the bus terminals take advantage of the natural confusion of the hundreds of people moving in every direction by offering to get you what you want faster and with less hassle. It's easy to take them up on their offer, especially when they say with such assurance that they can get you that seat on the bus to Baguio and the lady behind the window just told you the bus was full.

These guys do not work for anybody, although you may think they do. You can tell who works for the bus company and who doesn't. The employees usually have on a company shirt and wear shoes. The other guys who claim to be able to help you generally are wearing a dirty T-shirt and rubber slippers. They'll be the first ones to approach you, as they have trained themselves to spot that desperate look a mile away. They have also filled a gap, by putting themselves in position between the driver/conductor tandem, who are too busy smoking cigarettes, and you, the traveler in need.

The dirty T-shirt dude usually performs a non-paying task, like holding the door of the taxi which just dropped you off. I've also seen these guys help load the bus' luggage compartment. They assume you want a porter and grab your bags without asking. They work on the premise that once they so much as open the taxi door, or touch your bag, they are owed something because they helped you. They will also assure you that they can get you that desperately needed seat, which they will try to do if you let them.

But I've found that it's best to blow these guys off as they are doing nothing more than getting between you and what you want; that seat. I make it a point to go directly to the bus driver, take him around the back of the bus, and explain to him that I'd like to donate a gift to the boss's birthday party. The seat opens up, I'm off to Baguio and the dirty T-shirt guy is left looking for another pigeon.

In the rush to get a bus it is common to forget to buy some snacks or beverages. No need to worry, however, as a gap like hunger or thirst never stays open for long in Manila, especially on a public bus. At almost every stop, someone is climbing aboard selling their *chicharon* (fried pork skins), boiled quail eggs, peanuts or bottled water and sodas.

These people never fail to gain my admiration. They fry a few peanuts, place them in small, brown paper sacks and just stand on a busy street corner and wait for any of the thousands of rickety buses to pull over or get stuck there in traffic. Then they just climb aboard and sell their wares. Nobody tells them to be there, nobody licenses their work. Any money they make comes from pure unadulterated hustling.

The competition filling gaps on buses is fierce and strategy and positioning is everything. On the buses heading out to the provinces, there are legions of food sellers waiting for hungry and thirsty passengers at the various terminals and stops along the way. But they are often beaten out by the guys who hop aboard the buses at the exits and toll gates of the highways. Not only do these people fill the hunger and thirst gap

of the riding public, they fill the gap from the toll gate to the terminal. Call them double gap fillers.

Gap fillers and brokers have also set up shop at the North Harbor docks in Tondo. One time I came off the SuperFerry from the province and was confronted with what seemed like a pack of wild frothing land sharks just off the exit of the boat. These guys literally stand between you and the waiting cabs on the street.

"Taxi cab, sir? Taxi," they say hurriedly as they start following you without even waiting for an answer. Some will even grab your bags without you asking. These guys are not the taxi drivers. And unless you have somebody waiting to pick you up, they are almost impossible to get around, as they literally grab you by the arm and lead you to a cab.

If you don't like walking two kilometers for a taxi, you are nearly obliged to use their services. Actually they won't cost anything. It's the cabbies whom they seemed to have collared. Nobody uses the meter at the North Harbor, and the hustlers are setting the prices. They charge the cabbies a certain percentage up front before any passengers get into the taxi.

The weather often creates various gaps which never stay open for long. Some of my favorites are the window washers who appear out of nowhere at busy intersections as soon as it starts to rain. The gap here is created by the dirt and mud on the wet roads which flies up and on to people's windshields while they drive. The kids who fill this gap are some of the fastest gap fillers in town. One minute they are playing basketball on a dirt patch amidst the squatter shacks on the side of the road and, the next minute, as soon as the rain starts falling, they are sprinting barefoot through waiting traffic in a torrential downpour carrying a bucket and a sponge, washing windows for one peso a head.

There are literally hundreds of other examples in Manila of people filling gaps that society has left open. But why, you may ask, are there so many people engaged in brokering or gap filling? The answer is simple: pure unadulterated survival.

In rich countries, gap filling has long ago been made illegal. Yes, that's right, they actually made laws prohibiting the practice. It's called peddling and anyone engaged in peddling can end up in jail. If you want to go into business, you have to acquire all the appropriate licenses, closely follow strict rules and pay insurance and taxes. If not, you're expected to just go out and get a real job.

In the Philippines, and many other countries where millions of people are fighting for daily survival, there are way too many people and not enough real jobs to go around. Competition for survival is intense. In fact, there's not just competition from other humans, but from everything else including the dogs, cats, ants, rats and cockroaches. Every hour of every day, everyone and everything is competing for survival.

Gap filling is how people make work for themselves. They create things to do. They put themselves in position. There are no welfare handouts in the Philippines. No social safety net. No free meal kitchens. In the Philippines people often have to do some seriously creative things just to get a meal.

Working one parking spot can bring a meal in a matter of hours. Guaranteed. And in Manila they work it to the max. One little spot. That's all they need.

Never underestimate what these people do for the local economy. More than any real estate deal where the price of a piece of air doubles in a month's time, a few well-placed coins and notes are what actually keep the economy going. Because unlike many of the rich, who are really just rich on paper, gap fillers, brokers, and street hustlers go right out and spend their money.

And the people they spend it on, generally other marginal types who never get counted on any demographic charts, like owners of *carinderias* (canteens), *sari-sari* stores, jeepney drivers and *balut* vendors, also always go right out and spend the money.

So, like them or not, gap fillers help keep Manila operating and moving smoothly. Something to think about the next time you're in the big city and you're being hustled out on the streets.

A MARKET FOR EVERYTHING

It was just another Sunday, on just another weekend. Stuck in the dirty city and nothing going on. But it's amazing how Manila can sneak up and surprise you sometimes.

I woke up and decided I needed to have a mountain bike. I came to this conclusion when I discovered I had a little more than P5,000 in my shorts. I knew I needed to act quickly on my impulse, because, well, you know how it is with money. If you do not spend it quickly on what you want, it will soon become allocated for something else.

"Hey, where can I get a bike?" I asked my wife, Au. She thought for a few seconds and I interjected. "Just make sure it's not in a mall. I'm not going to any sterile mall just so I can feel like I'm back in America. Every time I go to these giant malls in Manila, I come out feeling like I just had a frontal lobotomy."

"I know," she said. "Let's go to Cartimar in Pasay City." I had never been to the Cartimar market before. I was a little surprised I hadn't heard about it before because I love markets and I never tire of checking them out.

I liked Cartimar even before we got out of the taxi. The driver took us down the sprawling Roxas Blvd., but then turned into a narrow lane and weaved his way through the crowded and dirty Pasay neighborhoods for a few minutes before dropping us off in a little city square.

This was definitely not a predictable mall.

Situated in Pasay City, down the street from Manila's teeming Baclaran area, and near the LRT train line, Cartimar gives off the air of a classic inner city market. The various businesses in Cartimar are lined up for several parallel blocks on the ground floor of old, low-rise buildings. The area where the market sits is semi-secluded and the noise from the traffic just a block away is nearly shut out. In the middle of total urban chaos, Cartimar is a place unto itself, with a rather cozy atmosphere to it.

Au told me that Cartimar was the kind of market where you can buy all kinds of things, some imported, some local, but that the prices there were definitely cheaper than the malls. There were bike shops aplenty and we dove right in. Forty-five minutes later, I got what I wanted.

I noticed a nice bike sitting chained up outside one shop and I asked the mechanic about it. Like all the other bikes, it was "made in Taiwan, with Japanese parts and assembled in the Philippines." He said it was one year old, that he was the one riding it and that it was worth P7,000 new but would take P5,500 now. I took it for a spin and decided it had my name on it. I sent Au in for the kill and got it for P4,500. A cyclist who had stopped by the shop to buy some parts noticed my new ride and nodded his approval.

"How much did you pay?" he asked.

"Four-five," I said.

"That's a good deal," he said. "If that were new that's P10,000." As he rode off I was beaming. There's nothing like the feeling when you got something you wanted and you got it at a good price.

With new bike in hand, we set out to explore the rest of Cartimar. Past several nice plant and orchid shops, Au honed in on a nondescript shop selling used clothes by the kilo. This was a first for my eyes. Ladies rummaged through the bins for bargains—P300 per kilo—and then brought their finds to the counter where the clerk weighed them on a scale like they were fruits and vegetables.

Cartimar is famous as a place to buy pets and this was fairly obvious from the amount of pet shops further down the street. However, these were unlike any pet shops I've ever seen. Dozens upon dozens of little shops stood lined up one after the next, selling every living creature imaginable; fish of every make by the thousands swam in small crowded tanks, purebred dogs including a basset hound, a pure white Japanese spitz, a boxer and scores of others sat in small cages waiting with sad eyes for a buyer, cages packed with hundreds of tiny white mice crawling all over each other, birds of every shape, size and color by the thousands, rabbits, turtles, monkeys, Tupperware buckets filled with hundreds of snakes crawling and writhing all over each other and even long giant green lizards that looked like they came straight out of the dinosaur age.

This scene had me agog. I had the feeling that the forests and oceans had been emptied of nearly all life, all in the name of profit. Apparently anyone can go into business selling anything they damn well please. The giant lizards had me wondering because I recalled seeing these very same lizards on a recent trip to Hawaii at the Honolulu Zoo. Except the lizards at the zoo were on display and not for sale and the placard next to their abode at the zoo explained how these lizards were very rare and nearly extinct.

Further down in Cartimar's pet section I came across another sight that stopped me in my tracks. An owl for sale. An owl? Owls are not the most plentiful of creatures and one doesn't normally see them in the marketplace. Amid the cacophony of barks and chirps

I spotted a weird looking monster sized fish in an
aquarium.

"Where's that big fish from?" I asked the store
owner.

"Argentina," he said. This piqued my interest, not
in an investigative way, but more in a wonderment
way. I had heard that these kinds of markets were
more wide open than the malls. "Wide open," meaning that you can sell just about anything. Also, you're
never quite sure the route by which the goods ended
up for sale there. The bikes could be seconds passed
off as new, the electronics could be slightly defective
and couldn't pass quality standards for Japan or the
States, the birds could be smuggled, the appliances
could have been stolen from a cargo ship in the Sulu
Sea. Of course, all or some of these products could very
well be the real thing.

I tried to imagine how those lizards ended up for sale.
Are people legitimately importing them? Hard to believe since they are definitely rare. Perhaps the lizards,
and many other things, are smuggled in by boat, even
little *banca* (outrigger) boats plying the waters between
Indonesia and Mindanao in the southern Philippines.
With over 7,000 islands, and a coast guard which could
reasonably defend no more than a few of the smaller
ones at one time, the Philippines is like a sieve which
is impossible to police. It would be easy to pull right
up on the beach with a few lizards, rare fish, boxes full
of stolen electronics or whatever goods happen to be
floating around out there.

Whatever the case, the scene at Cartimar had me
marveling at how Manila, and the Philippines in
general, is a place where a heck of a lot of goods pass
through. If you go around Manila and check out the
sheer amount of big markets you quickly start to realize that. At the sprawling and overflowing Divisoria

market in old Manila, block after block is given over to
every kind of product imaginable. From the smallest
button to the oddest color fabric to the most difficult to
find piece of hardware, Divisoria has it all. Truckloads
of food, locally produced goods and imported items, low
and high end alike, make the selection in Divisoria
mind boggling.

At the Baclaran market in Pasay, the streets and
alleyways are crammed with hordes of cheap clothes,
electronics and housewares, some locally made, others brought in from China. The heavily cramped and
dirty streets of Chinatown offer the impossible to find
spare part, every kind of hardware and endless jewelry
shops. The Cash and Carry Market in Makati carries
similar items to the Cartimar market but a tad more
upscale.

Those markets are but a mere sampling. What never
fails to amaze me is the breadth and scope of the market
in the Philippines. In the Philippines there is a market
for just about anything. Why is it that the seconds and
the slightly defective goods are always being dumped
in the Philippines? Because people will buy them.
If you don't know what to do with your goods, bring
'em to the Philippines. You're very likely to find your
market here.

One often hears criticism of the Filipinos' preference
for foreign goods being a symptom of their still lingering
colonial mentality. But the truth seems more like that
trading and goods coming and going are very much a
part of the cultural landscape of the country and have
been for a very long time. The Philippines has always
been a crossroads, a place where people have come to
trade. The Spanish galleons sailed to the Philippines
laden with silver looted from South America to meet
up with Chinese and Indian traders to trade for their
vases, spices and everything else. Today it's no dif-

ferent. From the duty-free shops, to the department stores, the supermarkets, the groceries, the weekly and monthly charity bazaars down to the neighborhood sari-sari stores and to the vendors and peddlers who walk up and down the streets, there is an incredible amount of trading and commerce taking place in the Philippines.

Which is also what I came to notice as I rode my bike through the clogged streets of the Baclaran area nearby Cartimar. Au had climbed into a taxi and, being in the market mood, we were to meet five kilometers away at the Parañaque Fresh Food Market out near the international airport. A bike in Manila puts you right in the middle of the chaos. On a bike you see, hear and feel everything. I dodged jeepneys, tricycles and kids pushing wooden carts laden with used bottles. I breathed in the foul air as jeepneys and old buses spewed their thick black soot right in my face. And I checked out the incredible amount of activity taking place.

Every nook and cranny of Baclaran seemed to be filled with people selling shoes, towels, electronics, fabric, furniture, whatever. I rounded the corner and headed down Taft Ave. under the LRT train and dodged people sprawled all over the streets and sidewalks selling fruits, vegetables and meats. Where there aren't people on the sidewalk, then it's piles of wood and garbage strewn about. I pedaled past dirty concrete, dilapidated buildings and stagnant streams of garbage. Ugliness for sure, but also bounty. If one only looked at the crumbling physical structure of Manila, the word 'dead' would be the first thing that came to mind. But in and around this seeming degradation, the city is really booming with a life of commerce and trading.

I arrived at the Parañaque Fresh Food Market ten minutes ahead of Au. But she showed up fresh and relaxed. I was relaxed from the exercise, but I was covered in filth. Literally, I could feel it. I could scrape it off my skin.

The Parañaque Fresh Food Market has been renovated over the last few years. A lot of people go there to buy their fish, meat and vegetables from the vendors, then take it over to one of the dozens of restaurants who will cook up a veritable feast for incredibly reasonable prices. It's a great place to sit and relax and watch the people go by and the arriving planes pass directly over head.

Which is exactly what we did. We lounged around, ate crabs, oysters, sashimi, drank a few cold San Migs and took in the scene. I love markets. The sounds, the colors, the smells, the activity. It makes me weak in the knees. A friend and fellow market lover once said to me, "Ted, life is in the marketplace." Indeed. There is so much that is core to life itself that you can just kick back, open up your mind and let it all come in.

Mostly I watched the parking lot dude with the big belly and the scraggly red hair. I've never seen anybody work a parking lot like this guy. With his whistle in hand he ran up and down the pavement frantically waving his arms, directing cars into spots or around to the back of the market, getting them out of tight spots and looking after little kids that were running around and making sure they stayed out of the way of any oncoming cars. He looked like a symphony conductor. His orchestra was the cars. He milked that parking lot to the bone and I saw he had a waist pack full of dough. I enjoyed his performance so much I gave him a P5 coin, even though I did not even have a car.

Later at home, covered in the filth of this sprawling, teeming and wild city, the phone rang and I smiled. For everything I had just been musing about was reflected in that phone. It was a cordless phone which I had just bought a week before. I had been thinking about buying a cordless phone when I happened upon a sidewalk sale of used phones and computers imported from the United States on display at a mall near my home. I bought that phone for a mere P900 and it worked perfectly. That's the way it goes in Manila. A market for everything and a surprise around every corner.

BIRD HUNTING

The call came in the middle of the day and with it came a familiar voice. My editor.

"I want to know if you're up for this one," he said. "Someone I know told me that there's this really wild and decadent bar somewhere in Manila where mostly expats go. This guy didn't even know the name of the place or where it is, but he said the place is like some known secret among the foreigners here. Have you ever been to this place or heard about it?"

"No," I said, "But you're telling me it's a secret place?"

"Well, sort of I think. Among foreigners. It's supposed to be a real hole in the wall. But supposedly anything goes right there in the bar. Are you interested in trying to find it and check it out?"

"What, a semi-secretive cheap dive frequented by sex-crazed expats? A place where decadence reigns? What do you take me for? Sure, why not. I'll see what I can dig up."

My first reaction after hanging up the phone was wondering why I hadn't heard of the place before. Oh well, I wasn't complaining. One can never get enough of the underbelly of life. While you'd have a hard time getting anybody to publicly admit there is any redeeming social value in cheap dives packed with decadent behavior, these kinds of places always offer up that bare bones honesty and no pretense action that so-called legitimate places could never give. There's a certain charm in things that are low.

What intrigued me, as well, was that not only was the place in question apparently semi-secretive, but it was also exclusive to expats. Expats in Asia have been known to go off the deep end and this one sounded like just that kind of spot.

But where to start? For several days I sat on the idea before finally, one dreary and rainy Friday night, I decided to venture out on a mission to find this dive whose name and location I did not even know.

I started in Makati at the Prince of Wales pub, a well-known watering hole frequented by the foreign crowd. I figured my chances were good someone at the Prince would have been to this place. I saw a friend who is a fellow scribe and pulled up a chair at the table where he, several foreigners, and their Filipina wives sat imbibing. When nobody was paying attention, I asked him about the cheap dive.

"That place?" he immediately asked in astonishment. "Why do you want to go there?"

"Because," I said, "I want to check it out."

"Oh man, that place is a real hole in the wall. The low of the low. You won't even be able to find it unless someone takes you there. It's in a real bad neighborhood." His friend Matt, a Welshman, had been sitting across the table and picked up what we were talking about. He moved his chair closer and joined the conversation.

"Matey, matey," he said laughing while shaking his head. "Talk about a dive. That place takes the cake." Both of them had been there at least once several years ago and for the next 45 minutes they filled me in on some of the details as they could remember them.

"These days it's sort of a traditional secret amongst foreigners," the scribe said. "But back in the 1940's,

after the war, that place used to be a society café. No
kidding. But over the years, especially during Vietnam,
it evolved into a sleaze joint."

"That's the understatement of the year," Matt said.
"They have a room next to the bar called 'The Office.'
That's where they conduct business, if you know what I
mean. When I went to this place, there was no sign, no
lights out front and no electricity. To get in you have to
knock on this big metal door. A slot opens and a pair of
eyes look at you. If they see you're all right, then they'll
let you in. When we walked in there was nobody there
and the place was dark. But all of a sudden, a bartender
comes out of nowhere with a cold San Mig, the piano
player turns up and sits at the old piano, they light a
few candles and put them on the piano and the girls
come over from the dorm across the street. You could
be the only one there and, no matter the time of day,
they'll open it for you."

"Sounds interesting," I said. "Why don't you take me
there?"

"I'm not even sure where it is, Matey," Matt said.
"Besides, I'm a happily married man." But I could tell
he was intrigued. The way he talked about the place, I
figured he had a good time there several years ago.

Thirty minutes later Matt and I were speeding
through the streets of Makati in his shiny black Honda
on our way to look for the joint. He had ditched his
wife at another Makati bar with some friends. Matt
had already had many drinks and drove like a crazy
man. He had only a vague idea where this place might
be. I also had had a few beers and soon lost my sense
of direction. I knew we were definitely no longer in
Makati. We must have driven for 45 minutes, mostly
in circles it seemed, through some of the darkest and
narrowest streets I have ever seen in Manila. Many of
the streets were torn up and the buildings looked old

and rundown. I figured this place's reputation must be well deserved.

We stopped several times to ask directions and soon started finding people who knew of the place. Finally we were directed to the exact location of the bar by a bicycle pedicab driver, who smiled when he pointed to the front door. Indeed the place was situated on a quiet, dark and narrow lane. Like every other building in the neighborhood the place looked run down. There were no lights on and there was no sign. We parked the car on the curb and the pedicab driver went to the front door and knocked. As Matt and I walked up, the door was slightly cracked open. When the woman inside saw the two foreigners, she opened the door all the way and let us in.

The first thing I saw were three white guys standing at the bar to my right drinking San Miguels. I heard them speaking German. They were surrounded by five attentive Filipinas wearing white T-shirts and shorts. The girls looked to be in their late teens and early 20's, except one who was easily in her 40's. None looked particularly pretty. A lady bartender sat behind the bar and an older lady, probably *Mamasan*, lounged on a chair against the wall. Other than that the place looked empty.

Matt and I sat at the bar and ordered two beers. The Mamasan suddenly recognized Matt. She remembered him from four years ago. I sipped my beer and looked around. The place had the unmistakable look of a dive that had not seen too much action in a while. Except for the chatter of the Germans and the Filipinas, the place was quiet with no music playing. A single bulb lit up one corner of the long bar and barely spread light around the rest of the room. Most of the corners were pitch black. Old dusty whisky bottles lined the shelf behind the bar. The wall in one corner was adorned with a calendar featuring naked Chinese girls.

"From a Swiss," Mamasan said, when she noticed us checking out the calendar. At the other end of the bar sat an idle piano. But what really caught my attention was the floor, which consisted of a maze of black and white painted tiles that when laid together formed what looked like one of those old M. C. Escher paintings that play tricks on the eye. The tiles were clean and in perfect condition. "That's the original floor," Mamasan said. Just then several new girls appeared out of nowhere and accosted Matt and me.

"Sir, what's your name?" asked one of the girls with an ugly grin.

"Joe," I said. "Hey, where's the piano player?"

"He's sleeping," said Mamasan. Suddenly a naked girl ran out of a dark area of the bar. She grabbed something from a table and ran back into the dark area.

"What's over there?" I asked Lucy, one of the girls who had swarmed over Matt and myself and who now had her hand placed between my thighs.

"That's 'The Office,'" said the bartendress.

"Sir, we go into The Office," Lucy said with a longing pout on her face.

"Why? What are we going to do over there?" I asked with a knowing smile. She stuck her tongue in her cheek and rolled it around. She laughed.

"How much for The Office?" I asked.

"P200 for The Office," Lucy said. "And you give me P400." I turned to Mamasan.

"Mamasan, I heard you can do anything at this place," I said.

"Sure, why not," she said smiling. "It's up to you." From The Office I heard a groan that sounded like it had a German accent.

"You mean anything?" I said. Matt had been sucking on his beer and chimed in.

"That's right matey," he said in a loud drunken voice. "You want 'em to dance naked on the bar? How much girls?"

"P100 each," said one of the girls. Matt and I reached into our pockets and each pulled out P100. We slapped the notes on the bar. Immediately two of the girls climbed up on the bar, stripped naked and started dancing.

"I like this place," Matt said loudly as he raised his beer. "A toast!!"

"Here, here," I said, also raising my beer. While the girls danced, the German appeared from The Office looking frazzled. He joined his friends at the bar and in a matter of moments they left. Only Matt and myself remained.

We ordered more beers while the two girls continued to dance and Lucy gave me a massage. The woman in her 40's approached me.

"Joe," she said, "how about I pick up coins with my *ano*?"

"Your what?" I asked.

"My *ano*," she said. "You know, my pussy."

"Oh, I see. Your *ano*. Sure, how much?"

"I pick up 50, 100 coins. It's up to you."

"Sounds like a deal," I said. Matt and I pulled out about P30 in coins and stacked them on the bar. The two girls climbed down from the bar and dressed. The woman got up on the bar and stripped naked. She had an ugly body but who cared. I wanted to see the peso-snatching *ano*. The bartendress placed an open baseball cap next to the coins. Then the woman squatted down upon the pile and, well, picked up the coins with her *ano* and dropped them in to the hat. Her deposits came down in two installments. It occurred to me that this is what they must mean by "dirty money."

While this was going on, a horny, shaggy brown mutt

of a dog walked around the room and jumped up on the leg of any woman he could corner. He attempted to screw the women but he couldn't reach. He only attempted this with the women.

"Is he just horny or is this some kind of performance?" I said looking towards Mamasan.

"He make butterfly just like you," she said with a big laugh.

"Where's the owner?" I asked her.

"She's not here," she said. "She's a Filipina and lives in San Francisco. She's married to a German."

When we got up to leave sometime later, several of the girls were asleep on the tables. The bartendress dozed in her seat. Mamasan said to come back again and bring some friends. Any time of the day, it did not matter.

"Remember you can do anything you want here," Mamasan said with a big smile. "And I mean anything."

"Yeh but next time," I said, "Make sure you wake up that piano player."

"No problem," she said with a laugh.

As Matt drove and we attempted to discover the quick route out of this neighborhood and back in to the late night Makati action, we talked excitedly about the joint. A dive, yes. A decadent hole in the wall, yes. But definitely not without its fair share of low-rent charm.

RIDING A BICYCLE IN MANILA

When I bought my mountain bike, those whom I told of my prized purchase automatically assumed that I would suddenly be hauling the bike out to the provinces where I'd be cruising up and down lush green hills, through gorgeous valleys and around shimmering bodies of water while enjoying fresh air and nature's beauty.

Yeh, sure sounds good. But haven't been there, haven't done that. Where I ended up using my bike was right in the teeming, car choked and polluted city of Manila. In fact soon after I bought it, my bicycle quickly became one of my favored modes of transportation. And this is not just for local trips down to the *sari-sari* store or the post office. I regularly ride my bike all over the city. Like from Parañaque, where I reside, all the way to the business district of Makati, a trip of some 8 km. Or down to the old Spanish walled city of Intramuros, a distance of over 12 km. Of course each one of these journeys is accompanied by a return trip.

Those Manileños who have learned of my use of a bicycle as a legitimate form of transportation throughout the metropolis, usually respond with something like this: "You what?" they exclaim with their jaw resting squarely on the floor. Then there's a brief silence and they just stand there with their head shaking back and forth. "You must be crazy." Well, there have been times......

For sure there are not too many of us on the roads.

There are a lot of kids riding their rusty BMX bikes from neighborhood to neighborhood. But the ones on long hauls never number more than a handful. Never have I seen more than a few. If we pass one another there's usually a casual glance followed by a nod of acknowledgment and understanding.

Sometimes you see cyclists in their cycling gear riding their racing bikes with the thin tires. I cannot understand how they survive Manila's awful roads with those thin tires. One has to literally have iron balls to ride a racing bike in Manila.

Belying its name, the mountain bike is actually the ultimate urban vehicle, allowing the rider a freedom the likes of which cars permitted in Manila twenty years ago, before they began to turn on their owners and systematically enslave the entire populace. A mountain bike allows me to travel via the main roads, service roads, sidewalks and any other path. I ride right past all motorized vehicles, which sit and wallow in the constant gridlock. I cut in and around traffic. I ride on the sidewalk. I ride the wrong way down a one way street. I even run red lights. Bikes are given total leeway in Manila. A person on a bike can do as he pleases. Cops and traffic enforcers have yet to say a word to me. Usually they just stare in befuddlement, probably wondering about the sanity of the crazy foreigner. If they did want to give chase, I could easily out run them as I have much greater mobility than they do. And I never have to worry about a place to park. I pull right up to wherever I'm going, lock the bike to a post, do what I have to do and then I'm off.

On a mountain bike, I can easily get around much faster than a car in Manila. The ride from Parañaque to Makati takes me 40 minutes. Using a car or public transportation could also take 40 minutes, but only if every single person in the city came down with the flu on the exact same day and called in sick to work. On an ordinary business day, that same trip by car would more than likely take one hour, perhaps one hour and a half. Yeah, I arrive hot as hell, perspiring like Pagsanjan Falls and stinking to high heaven. But what do I care? Usually I'm just running errands. Does it matter what the teller at the bank thinks of my latest cologne, Eau de Traffic? So long as the check cashes, right? Anyway, I like the exercise. Which, I have to admit, is no doubt completely offset by the amount of heavy exhaust fumes that a bicyclist in Manila tends to inhale. I wear a handkerchief over my nose and mouth, but the poisons released into the air in Manila by the rickety old buses and jeepneys could penetrate a ten foot, reinforced steel wall.

People often tell me I'm nuts because they assume riding a bicycle around the city is dangerous. I won't lie to you and say it's all a piece of cake. But it's not as bad as you think.

It's all attitude. The surest way to an accident is to go out there and be timid and try and hide from the rampaging cars, buses and jeepneys, all of whom so courteously follow one law—the law of the jungle. They'll run you off the road in a New York second, and that means in a hurry. On a bike you have to make yourself known. You have to put yourself out there for all to see. Because while the driving habits of Filipinos are generally atrocious, Filipinos are, nonetheless, quite defensive drivers. Anybody who drives a car in Manila knows that. What's amazing is that amidst all the utter bedlam on the roads, there are far less car accidents in Manila than one might expect. This is not because drivers have any overriding concern about me or any other fellow human being. It's just that they are terrified about getting a scratch on their car. God forbid a Filipino gets a little scratch on his car! Also they do not want to hit you because then they'd have to pay out a tidy sum of pesos which they don't have because it's all been sunk into their precious automobile.

However, you can never let your guard down. Just like when you're driving a car, a bicyclist automatically assumes that everyone else on the road is a complete schmuck. (That's 'jerk' for those uninitiated in the yiddish language.) There are times I'm pedaling down a busy road when I wish that my little bike were actually a giant Sherman tank. I especially get this urge when a guy backs out of a spot without even looking, or someone darts from a side road on to the main road without so much as slowing down to look, or when a jeepney cuts me off while pulling over into the middle of the road to stop and drops off a passenger. This happens often, forcing me to hit the breaks, where I then have to make a split second decision to either swerve left into the road and possibly an oncoming bus, or swerve right towards the curb and possibly jump off and abandon the bike.

Oh, how deliciously wonderful it would be to be able to instantly become a ferocious tank rumbling down the road! As soon as the jeepney driver rudely cuts me off, I yell *"Bayad Po!!"* (I'd like to pay, please.) Upon hearing the familiar refrain from one of his customers, the driver turns around to collect the money, but instead of coins, he gets a mouthful of heavy iron treads that proceed to crush his jeepney and him into a mash of metal, flesh and bone road kill for all to see. Sick, yes but, like I said, you tend to develop an attitude while riding a bicycle in Manila.

You also develop a strange sense of wonderment. Manila is in a constant state of utter chaos and flux. Several times during any long ride I invariably come across scenes that are beyond normal human comprehension. I often find myself shaking my head and murmuring things like, "This is the road from hell!" or "Oh man, this is the intersection from hell!"

It's the combination of the incomprehensibly massive construction projects at every turn combined with way too many people and cars. It gets even more mind boggling when the weather turns astoundingly hot, which it seems to do on a regular basis. Together Manila has the appearance of a future gone mad scenario, a phenomenon so crazed and depraved they won't even put it in the movies.

There's nobody in Manila who hasn't seen all this, but sitting inside an air conditioned car with tinted windows and love songs blaring out endlessly from the stereo tends to insulate you from reality. On a bicycle, you literally hear and feel this city.

One tortuously hot day during El Niño, I'm riding my bicycle on one of Parañaque's service roads on my way home when I encounter what appears to be total gridlock extending two kilometers. Without stopping I ride my bicycle in and out of the idling cars. At times there is no room to move so I have to jump off the bike and carry the bike over a stump on the side, or around a tree. I do not mind this because even though I am incredibly overheated, at least I am still moving. That's the beauty of a bike.

At one point I am walking with the bike and I just stop and look at the scene around me. As hellish as it can get, I think. There can be nowhere on earth with a scene equal to this. Roads jammed with cars idling, stuck in another traffic snarl, going absolutely nowhere fast. Everywhere a conflagration of rubber, concrete, burning gas, hot oil, hot metal rubbing against hot metal, rubber melting on the radiating concrete. The heat feels like a furnace as it amplifies off the mash of metal, off the pavement, off the tops of idling cars and trucks. Wherever I look I can see trash piled and scattered, trash that's been there so long it's been burned into the thirsty brown scraggly grass.

In between the trash, lay piles of scrap wood, surrounded by walls of hot twisted tin sheeting adorned with torn and tattered posters of smiling politicians dangling in the hot and still air. In any direction I take my gaze I see industry, high concrete walls with twisted and rusted barbed wire and rusted water tanks shooting up in to the sky. Off to one side I can see the South Super Highway. The northbound lane looks like a parking lot. Above the snarl an army of guys helping to build the new Skyway climb all over the large metal scaffolding erected over the road, attacking a mammoth concrete pylon while exposed to the relentless sun and every known poison in the world simultaneously. On the southbound side of the highway, second hand, smoke belching buses with Chinese lettering on the sides spew their bile into the thick hot air. Near the pylons, cement trucks churn round and round. Then a piercing wail fills the air and I see a heavy and rickety old train belonging to the Philippine National Railroad lumber by on the nearby tracks. It's then I notice people living amidst and on top of this scene. Ramshackle squatter shacks line both sides of the tracks. Near the road, several hot and bored looking people sit on stoops watching over their sari-sari stores selling old breads, chips, candies. In some stores they display cooked food in metal trays that sits and wallows in the heat inside a glass box, waiting for a hungry soul to stumble by and take his chances.

I drag my hand across the back of my neck, slightly digging my nails into my wet skin. My hand comes away dripping wet and my nails are filled with wet black dirt. I am alarmed and fascinated at the enormity of this scene and I wonder, "What has mankind wrought upon the world? What is the end result of all this chaos

and anarchy? Where is all this heading? This must be
what hell looks and feels like!"

For sure there's a certain amount of pride in being
able to deal with this hell, like a badge of honor just for
having to put up with it, to say I lived through it. But
it's nothing to brag about and in a minute I am gone.
Back on my bike, cruising in and out of the idling cars
and jeepneys, happily leaving them all in my extremely
hot, dusty and sweaty wake.

"If you go to the States," says Buboy, "it means you're richer, with better breeding. It means you're cool. One guy said he just came back from four months in the States. He was acting all cool. Like he's a 'G.' He was calling himself Frankie Holmes. But we found out he'd never even been to the States."

THE PIG IN THE SIDECAR

Amidst the daily collision of too many humans and industrial chaos, the ever growing grime and garbage, the quickly rising prices where you get no better service or standards, the lousy economy which is lousier than officials even dare to admit, the tortuous heat that just will not seem to go away, the incredible traffic phenomenon which everyone knows will get worse and worse, the instances of wild crime which constantly appear to be creeping closer and closer to home you do, occasionally, come across scenes in the city of Manila which in themselves are so very priceless that you just have to break down in utter laughter and tell yourself, through the chuckles and guffaws that, yes, only in this city could one witness something so outrageous and yes, living in Manila does indeed have its moments.

When the incident to which I am referring actually happened before my stunned eyes, I could not stop relating the story to anyone who would listen. What I found interesting was that even Filipinos, jaded by entire lives surrounded by outrageous happenings and goings on, even found it extremely funny.

The story begins with a very large pig. Probably the largest pig I have ever laid eyes on. This swine was a massive, hairy, pink beast that, with a few more pounds and a horn jutting out of its forehead, could have easily been mistaken for a rhinoceros.

I saw this giant rhino-pig while I was sitting in a
jeepney on a weekday afternoon while stuck in another
choking traffic snarl, this one along the Alabang-Zapote
road in the southern part of the metropolis. I was the
lone passenger in the jeepney and, at the time—around
three thirty in the afternoon—I had been staring out
the low window of the jeepney at the chaotic scene going on around me. The Alabang-Zapote road, right at
the turnoff to the province of Cavite, was, at the time,
one of those intersections that belonged in a future
gone mad scenario like in the movie Blade Runner. The
amount of construction, dust, garbage and traffic all
combined with the soaring heat radiating off of huge
solid slabs of concrete and metal from the new but not
totally complete highway-flyover, could have qualified
this hateful place as the number one intersection from
hell in Metro Manila, which is saying quite a lot.

Anyway, the jeepney was going nowhere fast, just
idling in traffic like you often do in Manila for twenty
minutes without moving an inch. The driver was attempting to make a left turn off the main road and
go down a side street. This seemed to complicate our
situation, because, of course, traffic was also going
nowhere fast in the other direction. In other words, we
were caught in total gridlock.

I was sitting there eyeing this very normal Manila
type scene and wondering, as I like to do, about the
sanity of the human race and how it came to be that
cars have managed to become the masters of the people
when it should be the other way around, when, out
of the corner of my eye, I saw the pig. He pulled up
alongside of the jeepney and also wanted to make a left
turn. I don't mean to say the pig was driving a car or
anything like that. No, the pig was being carted along
by two young guys riding a motorcycle.

The motorcycle had a big metal barred sidecar attached to it and the pig was literally stuffed inside the side car. The side car was rather large and yet it could barely hold this massive beast. It was as if the pig had been stuffed inside the car by some kind of packing machine. His snout was jammed between two narrow bars in the front, gobs of pig flesh spilled out through the open bars on the side, and his giant pig butt protruded over the top of the back bar. The pig wiggled and writhed furiously but it was clear he was not going anywhere except to the slaughterhouse. Or somebody's back yard. Same thing, really.

As you can imagine this scene managed to yank me

out of my musings about industrial Armageddon and fully grab my attention. It's one thing to see the humans amidst all their mess, but to see a giant pig cruising along in the middle of a business district just seemed, well, interesting, to say the least.

Then as we continued to wait to make a left turn that seemed like it would never happen, the pig began to urinate right in the middle of the road. Now a big pig does not know how to urinate like Filipino guys, who can manage to pee against a brick wall in public and make it look to all passersby like they are merely reading the graffiti. No, a pig doesn't know about trying to conceal anything. He just lets it fly. And it's not a little stream either. It's more like a fire hose.

So here is this incredibly massive pig shooting a water cannon of pee all over the Alabang-Zapote road right in the middle of rush hour in front of God and everybody. The pig peed for what seemed like a minute and I started to become worried, what with all the construction and everything, that the area might soon become flooded and we'd never get out of there.

It takes a lot to faze Filipinos but I noticed that many had turned their attentions to the urinating pig. The jeepney driver was laughing as were dozens of people over towards the side of the road. Even the traffic cop had a smile on his face. The two guys on the motorcycle could do nothing but laugh to themselves.

Eventually the pig drained his bladder but he wasn't finished with the show yet. Oh no sir. He looked neither comfortable nor happy stuffed inside that sidecar and he was going to give the humans, for whom he would soon be a meal, a piece of his, well, ... it wasn't his mind, let's just say that.

Finally a space opened up in the other lane and the traffic cop cleared us to turn. The motorcycle to our side inched ahead and as it started to turn, this giant massive pig, with his big pig butt sticking out over the back of the side car, started to let it fly. As the motorcycle slowly turned left, the pig dropped clump after clump of massive pig crap right on the pavement. The two guys on the motorcycle just kept moving and our jeepney followed right behind as the pig left a long curving trail of crap right in the heart of the Zapote business district. Inches from the stunned cop, inches from the bumper of a brand new Toyota, inches from the sidewalk next to a 24-hour Uniwide convenience store.

The motorcycle and its suddenly relieved cargo found open road and sped away, after leaving the people of Zapote a noxious gift maybe 15 meters long. I recall my jaw had fallen open. At the same time I laughed hysterically. I had already been marveling at the out of control urban scene around me and now a pig the size of a bull comes along and poops all over the intersection. As we made the turn, I noticed that a lot of people had also caught the pigs last act and were also either laughing, looking on in amazement or both.

Indeed, the whole thing defied explanation, description, rationale. A super huge pig, crammed inside a metal barred sidecar, emptying his bowels in the middle of town on a busy day and managing to stun a populace not easily moved by even the craziest of happenings.

I don't know whose table that pig ended up on, but I can definitely say this; he sure as heck went out with a big bang didn't he?

FINE BABES AND
ALTERED STATES

The Jumbo Grill *Ihaw-Ihaw* restaurant in the Ermita section of Manila is one of those big, open air places whose noise, smoke, action, crowd and busy atmosphere make it hard to resist. It is Friday night and, as one might expect, the place is packed. Tonight I am out with the young Filipino crowd. Buggy, 17, and Adrian, 18, are brothers. Jun, their friend, is 19. Buboy is the eldest at 21. Together they like to call themselves "The *Bata* Boys." The fifth member of this clique, Daddy Pee Wee, 17, couldn't make it tonight.

They are relatives of my wife and I have been asked to take the boys out for the night. Perhaps my wife thought we might play billiards. Instead I have brought them here for some beer and *pulutan* (drinking snacks). Guys this age don't normally walk into a place like this, and I can see that they are excited. Of course they know that I'm buying tonight.

"This place is cool," says Jun. "We like it here." They are your regular teenagers from middle class families who are at that age when they are no longer kids, but not quite yet adults. Not too sure of themselves, more than a bit naive and not particularly ambitious, they like to slack off and watch cheap videos at friends' houses, play billiards, eat junk food, listen to music, go to clubs and be lazy.

I call over the waiter and order a round of beers, a pack of Marlboro for the boys and some pulutan—*ki-*

lawin (tangy raw fish), sticks of pork barbecue and sizzling *sisig* (chopped pig's ears, mouth, tongue, belly, etc.). The conversation starts to flow. They start asking me about America. None of them has ever been there, but they'd like to go if they get the chance. They are curious and it quickly becomes apparent to me that when many Filipino teenagers look at their future, however bleak they think it might be, they see themselves in the States. And what they see in the States are dollars.

"We don't understand something," Buggy asks me. "Why did you come here to the Philippines? I mean, your earning power is so much better in the States isn't it?"

"Yeh that's true," I say, wondering if earning power is the only barometer of happiness. "But your spending power is greater too. You have to pay for everything in the States. That's what America is all about. Money. And you better have a lot of it if you're going there."

"We don't like the Philippines anymore," says Jun, as the waiter brings the beers, the kilawin, the barbecue sticks and a pack of 'Boros. "I want to go to America."

"Do you know that if you were in the States right now," I say, "you wouldn't be sitting here with me in this restaurant drinking beer and smoking cigarettes? Because it's illegal. You can't drink unless you are 21 or over. And they are strict."

"Oh that's not cool. I think I like the Philippines."

"Yeah, the Philippines is loose compared to the States," I tell him. "You can do a lot of stuff here you can't do in the States. Don't turn your back on this country."

"But I want to go to the States to meet Alicia Silverstone," Jun says with a big smile. "I have a crush on her. And also Sharon Stone, Drew Barrymore and Demi Moore."

"That's why guys want to go to the States," Buboy chimes in. "To meet a lot of fine babes."

I wonder if anyone has informed them that all these "fine babes" in the States won't exactly be waiting at the arrival gate for them when they get off the plane in San Francisco. Or that out-of-work, teenage Filipino immigrants are hardly considered "hot items" on the dating circuit in the States. Evidently it wouldn't make a difference even if they were told about these potential downsides.

Nearly fifty years of American colonization in the first half of the 20th century, near economic colonization ever since, as well as two huge military bases have left the Filipino psyche focused in one direction: America. Filipinos are lured to America by everything around them from the time they are born. Kids grow up seeing relatives going off to the States. They hear the stories when they come back. They hear very tall tales from friends lucky enough to have gone already.

On top of this they are inundated with an endless line of slick ad jingles which invoke everything great as coming from America: Products are "an American classic," or "an American tradition." They promise the "taste of the USA," or, as with Winston cigarettes, "the Spirit of the USA." Koronets is "the great American snack." While the cheap, Made in China, disposable razor offers "that great American shave!"

For most Filipino teens, though, the excitement of America is generated by watching B-rated Hollywood action videos that feature the latest Porsche and Harley Davidson, hot women and easy money. It all leads to the easy conclusion; anyone able to get to America can simply get any job they want, make big money and score those "fine babes."

The waiter delivers a sizzling plate of sisig and I order another round of beers.

"What would you earn per day at a McDonald's in the Philippines?" I ask the boys. This is how you compare countries and the state of their economies these days—by the amount of money paid by multinational fast food joints to their employees.

"Around P150 a day," says Adrian.

"That's about what you earn in one hour at a McDonald's in the States."

"In one hour?" he says.

"In pesos it comes out to about P18,000 to P20,000 a month, after taxes. Can you deal with that?"

"Oh yeah. I'd take that any day," says Adrian. "That's good money."

"But that's starvation wages in the States," I say. "Wait till some first-world poverty hits your butt. You'll be dying to come back to the Philippines. It's a cold world in America. It'll eat you up and spit you out."

"But we've seen pictures," says Buggy, as the waiter places a beer in front of him. "Some of our friends came back from the States with photos. They said everybody's got money there. It's easy to get a job that pays big money."

"Who said that?"

"This guy Charlie. He showed us pictures of a Jeep he said he owned, and his two Mercedes and a house."

It does not take me long, though, to find out that Charlie is a fraud. A 24-year-old Filipino who had grown up in Los Angeles and who cleans carpets for a living, Charlie had come to the Philippines under the guise of returning to his roots. But what he was really doing in Manila was trying to get laid and act cool. Bragging about how rich he was and acting tough. Dropping names and places that Filipino kids know from the movies. Using his American "hipness" to impress everyone, especially the girls. Turns out he's always broke in the Philippines and sponges off his girlfriend's family to survive.

"Did you ever wonder why he was broke if he claimed to have all this money and cars?" I ask.

"No we didn't think of that," Buggy says sheepishly. There are legions like Charlie. Some have grown up in America. Others have been there for only a few months. It doesn't matter. Apparently just having set foot on American soil is enough to make one "the man" among today's Filipino youth.

"If you go to the States," says Buboy, "it means you're richer, with better breeding. It means you're cool. One guy said he just came back from four months in the States. He was acting all cool. Like he's a 'G.' He was calling himself Frankie Holmes. But we found out he'd never even been to the States."

Buboy explains that a "G" is a gangster, something that many kids fancy themselves as these days. They discovered Frankie was lying when they realized his gangster accent sounded just like a Visayan accent.

"He was acting like he's the boss," Buboy says. "Trying to impress the kids. He knows a lot of shit from the States that he learned from some of his *balikbayan* friends."

Then there's 17-year-old Daddy Pee Wee, the fifth member of the "Bata Boys," and, it seems, the leader of the group. Pee Wee's family is loaded, and Pee Wee lives by himself in a condo on Roxas Blvd. His father sent him to the States last year to go to school. After a year he came back to the Philippines.

"Now he acts like he doesn't speak Tagalog anymore," says Buggy. "His father gives him all the money he wants and Pee Wee spends money for us. That's why we call him Daddy Pee Wee. He's like our father. He takes us out."

"Why did he come back to the Philippines?" I ask.

"He said he got in some trouble there," says Buboy.

"He claims he killed a lot of people in the States. But he acts like a kid. We don't believe him."

"Pee Wee's a good man," says Buggy. "He just wants to see us happy. Wants us to brag about him. Tell the boys how big time he is." They inform me that Pee Wee drives a Lite Ace van, which basically puts him on top of the social heap in Manila.

"Here in the Philippines," says Jun, "if you have a car, you have everything. Especially if it has a big stereo system. Even if you're ugly you get all the fine babes. People would exchange their house and live in a shanty just for a fine car."

"And some Filipinos," says Buggy, "they carry their cell phones even though the phone doesn't work."

"Why is that?" I ask.

"Because they want to impress people," says Buboy. "Filipinos are social climbers."

I order another round of beers and we converse for a while longer. As the crowd starts to thin, the "Bata Boys" tell me they have to get going. I call for the check. I now realize how confusing life must be for many Filipino kids in their late teens and early twenties. They are caught at an age when they face the pressure of being cool and the pressure of life's coming realities. And the reality is that to be "somebody," it's better that they leave their country and go to the States. Other than that, they should just pretend.

"It's all status quo," says Buboy as I settle the bill. He meant to say, "It's all status," but I get his point. No wonder these boys would rather chill out.

"HEY JOE, WELCOME TO TONDO"

There are not too many places in Manila, or for that matter in the Philippines, that have as bad and as sordid a reputation as Tondo. To many, just the mere mention of the word brings forth visions of unfathomable urban squalor to the nth degree. Speak Tondo and you speak of the poorest of the poor, the ghetto of ghettos, of impossible crowds, of violence and danger lurking around every dark corner, of random street fights, of Manila's mean streets, of guys too poor to buy guns but nonetheless stalking the filthy and crowded boulevards and narrow lanes with *bolo* knives, butterfly knives and bows and arrows looking to knock off unsuspecting and innocent citizens.

And, indeed, as you head into Tondo, it has all the trappings of the evil of which people speak. Coming from Roxas Boulevard you bid good-bye to the green grass of the Intramuros golf course like it's an old friend. For as soon as you get to the top of the bridge, it hits you square in the face. The dirty North Harbor on the left. On the right the tin patched shacks, shanties and boxes that serve as people's homes, piled on top of one another, looking as if one stiff breeze will send all crashing to the ground, grimy little half naked kids running amidst piles of garbage, crowds of people so thick you'd think they were an army of teeming ants.

Normally I do not find myself hanging out in Tondo. However, one Saturday I had been called to announce a pro boxing match there. I was sitting in a taxi with my American friend, Levi, checking out this very scene. With the windows down. The windows were down because Levi had to have a smoke. It had taken us 45 minutes to get to Tondo from Parañaque. Levi cannot go that long without a puff. These days anyway. He's found himself living in a Parañaque barrio, got all of P3,000 in the bank and his wife is seven months pregnant. So I understood the need for a cigarette.

"Man do you know that the price of a pack of locally made Marlboro went from P16 to P18 in the last week and a half?" Levi said as he pulled one out of his shirt pocket, lit it up and rolled down the window. "So now on the street the price of a single Marlboro has gone from one peso to P1.25. Check this out. They disappeared from the shelves at 7-11 for two days last week. You couldn't even buy them. And when they came back they were P18 a pack. I'm telling you man, it was like the supplier suddenly demanded more money and the

people at 7-11 balked at paying the price. But then they must have caved in and paid the new price and so now the price is up. Isn't that somethin'? The supplier held back the shipment just when there was all this talk of economic chaos. You know how much money they must've made? Unreal. I tell ya man, that's slick."

While Levi cursed the price hike in his nasty habit, I soaked up the grime from outside. It hadn't rained in months and the Tondo night was sultry and thick with darkly colored foul air. As the taxi turned right, away from the harbor and into the fray, the crush of humanity became nearly impossible to comprehend. People were everywhere moving in every possible direction. The cab lingered in the squall and I contemplated this scene peculiar to third world urban centers; all of life taking place right out in the open; a barber shop in an open closet on the side walk, a baker operating in a corner hovel, a guy peeing behind a parked jeepney, people selling barbecue on a rickety grill right on the street, a blanket and a pile of shoes on the sidewalk for a shoe store. And even blood in the streets!

No, this was not the blood of humans. This was the blood of pigs being slaughtered right on the streets. Forget about the market, these pigs were being killed right on the pavement in front of God and everybody.

"Man we definitely live in the Third World," I said to Levi. "Check that out." A big, bloody pig carcass lay split wide open and spread eagle on a wooden table. The guy who had just killed the swine minutes before stood over the lump of pink flesh, blood dripping off his shirt and hands. Next to the killing table, five pigs, still alive, stood crammed inside a cage on the pavement, only minutes away from the same deadly and bloody fate as their friend.

There must have been thousands of people hanging and moving around the area and they all seemed to be laughing and having a good time. But of course they were. I noticed the colorful plastic streamers hanging over the streets and the sign that read "Viva Sto. Niño." I suddenly realized the reason for all the merriment. This was no ordinary Saturday night in Tondo. It was the start of the annual Tondo town fiesta.

People were out in force, heading to the houses of relatives and friends where they would eat and drink for free. A mass of humanity, vast and endless, out to have fun in the crowded and now bloody streets of Tondo. El Niño be damned. Sto. Niño had won the hearts of Tondo folk. As the cab worked its way through the throng, several bicycle pedicab drivers leaned in the open window.

"Hey Joe where you going?" one said with a smile.

"Hey Joe welcome to Tondo," said another as they all laughed. Indeed I was kind of psyched. What fiesta would be complete without a beauty contest, a cock fight and a boxing match?

The crowd on Masinop St. was so thick that the taxi couldn't move and we had to stop a block short of the boxing arena. Across the street from Tondo high school, the semi-covered Plaza basketball court was packed with people. For sure Levi and I were the only foreigners there and we felt like the only foreigners in the world. That is until we were warmly greeted by the local city councilor, Salo Gonzales, who was one of the local officials responsible for the night's action, which was free to the public. Levi found a front row seat in the VIP section, along with various local celebrities and politicians.

You've heard of an SRO crowd—standing room only. Well this was on the next level of crowd descriptions; HRO—hanging room only. Actually there wasn't even much of that left. They were hanging off the rafters. They were sitting in tall trees, crowded on to iron barred balconies and on to tin roof tops a block away just to get a glimpse of the fisticuffs.

The night got started with a few young amateurs, who looked like they had just walked out of the crowd. They were young teenage kids who wore protective cups on the outside of their dirty shorts and no shoes or socks. When the bell rang, they flailed at each other like two crazed alley cats and the crowd went wild. No matter that the skill level of these kids rated a minus two on a scale of one to ten. Filipinos love a good war. They love when two guys bang. They love drama. They love courage, blood and guts.

When the pros hit the ring they got all of that and more. Eight fights took over four hours to complete and not one person left his ringside seat or lamp post. Including Levi. Afterwards he was smiling ear to ear. He had come with P400 in his pocket and, at the end, he had P1,300 He had bet on all eight fights and won every single one of them.

It was past midnight when the boxing ended. Levi and I walked through the still crowded streets of Tondo. Thousands of young people stood crowded around a stage area watching eight six year olds, wearing matching white shirts and checkered skirts, gyrate to the latest sounds blaring over the overly loud speakers.

"I'm a Barbie girl," the song screamed, *"in my Barbie world. Wrapped in plastic, it's fantastic. You can comb my hair, undress me anywhere. Imagination, that is your creation. Come on Barbie, let's go party. Ooohh, oooohh, ooooohh, yehhh. Come on Barbie let's go party....."*

We weaved our way through the crowds and took in the stares and silly laughs.

"Hey Joe, where you going?"

"Hey Joe, high five. Alright man!! Where you from?"

Down the block we pulled over at a sari-sari store for

a couple of ten peso San Miguel beers. Levi explained his highly scientific method of picking the winners.

"Cause I noticed he had a bunch of fans in the audience," he said when I asked why he chose his particular bet in the fourth fight of the night. Of another one of his winners he said, "The guys at ringside were saying that the dude broke his thumb a week and a half ago in the gym. I figured any guy who steps into the ring with a broken thumb, gotta be some kind of tough." Of another winner he said, "Because he looked intelligent when he climbed up the ring." Or how about this gem: "I liked the stars going down the side of his shorts."

As we headed over the bridge in the taxi out of Tondo, with the tops of rusting shipping containers to our right, and the rusting rooftops of the Tondo ghetto to our left, Levi rolled down the window and lit up a Marlboro. As the humid, dirty air filled the cab, he reached into his pocket and pulled out his winnings.

"Man, Sunday I gotta pay rent," Levi said looking at his wad of cash. " I just made rent."

"You like Tondo, don't you?" I said.

"Yeah, I do," he said. And we both laughed.

THE PARTY IN THE PARK

The late afternoon sun casts its soft glowing light, making an already beautiful setting nearly picture perfect. Manicured rolling green lawns spread out in every direction. Big beautiful trees, their leaves swaying in the warm breeze, stand watch over the fertile landscape. A fountain bursts forth in the middle of a small tree lined lake. A cloudless sky emits a rich blue color.

And there is activity amidst the tranquility. Caretakers, some young, some old, but each a dark chocolate brown, no doubt from long days out in the sun, crouch under big colorful umbrellas, accompanied by the sound of their hand clippers moving back and forth as they trim the grass. A family walks down a foot path, carrying bottles of Coke, plastic tubs of food, a blanket and a guitar. Another family has gathered around a tree. The father and his two daughters toss a ball back and forth, while mom sits in a chair eating. Nearby another family has spread out their things. Two kids play badminton while the parents light a barbecue.

No doubt a perfect scene. As good as it gets anywhere. But I bet you didn't guess that I am sitting inside a cemetery, in particular Manila Memorial Park in Parañaque. It is several days before Nov. 1st, All Souls Day, and Manila Memorial is starting to burst with activity as people come early to clean the gravesites of their relatives. Come Nov. 1st, this place, along with cemeteries throughout the Philippines, will be packed with Filipinos visiting the graves of their loved ones. Shakey's Pizza trucks and portable Jollibee restaurants will pull up and Filipinos will come and stay overnight with their dead relatives and do the things that the dead used to like to do when they were alive. They'll play a few games, hang out, perhaps pass around a bottle of rum, light up a barbecue, talk story and gossip. Whatever they can do to make the dead feel comfortable and at home. Definitely a uniquely Filipino custom.

I find it amazing how Manila Memorial feels more like a public park, or a fancy subdivision, than a cemetery. The atmosphere—beautiful terrain, combined with families practically frolicking beside the graves of their relatives—is not just serene, but nearly pleasant. The hundreds of large stone mausoleums can easily be mistaken for houses or condos. There's a nice paved road around the park. They even have a little garden area where they keep monkeys and eagles.

However, certain sights serve to remind you of exactly where you are. A small tractor with a wagon attached onto the back pulls up to a plot. Three men get off and begin to unload a cement tomb. Once the tomb is sitting on the ground, they pull out their shovels and begin to dig, getting the moist fertile land ready for another body.

Then I start looking at the headstones. They hint at so many stories, many lives that have, in their own small way and in such a brief time, brought the world to where it is today.

While you see many people who lived to be old—in their 70's, 80's and 90's—I'm struck by the fact that there are many in the Philippines who die so very young. I see one lady who died at only 32 years old. Another lady who died at 41, another at 38. One baby lived for just two days, another for two months. I come upon brothers, one 41, the other 38, buried in the same plot.

Headstones on graves give no indications of how the person died. Just simple phrases; "We love you mommy." "You will forever be enshrined in our hearts." "Here lies the vessel of her soul... but her spirit lives in our hearts forever." Religious phrases asking the Lord for eternal peace.

Still, the setting here is almost too incredibly peaceful and majestic and I begin to wonder if there's more here, something else going on—if you'll pardon the pun—beneath the surface. Surely, I think, there must be some odd stories in here, things that cannot be explained. After all, almost every Filipino I've ever met has said they've seen ghosts, or at least they believe that ghosts are real.

I ask one caretaker if he has come across any ghost stories at the park. He smiles.

"I once saw a cross moving around at night," he says. I wonder if he really saw the cross moving. Or perhaps, I thought, this ghost had jumped out of a bottle of Ginebra Gin, which he had drunk after a long, tiring day of taking care of graves. I imagine it would be easy to convince yourself you saw a ghost, especially after drinking that swill.

I ask the two security guards watching the main gate if they've ever seen a ghost inside the park. They laugh.

"No," says the one, "this is a quiet park. I've been working here almost one year and I've never seen anything like that."

I wander over to an area where they keep the urns of people's ashes. There I meet Boy, a caretaker. He points across the lake and says that in 1994 he saw four carabaos walking on the banks of the lake. It was the middle of the day. There are no carabaos in Manila

Memorial, he said. The carabaos wandered behind some trees. He went over to find them and they had disappeared. To this day he's convinced it was some sort of ghost.

I sit down on the grass under a tree beside several plots. I start talking to Luis Opeña, an old caretaker who is resting nearby. Like the other caretakers here, he's thin and dark brown. He tells me he's 48 years old and I'm surprised because he looks older than his years. He says he's been a caretaker for 10 years. I ask him if he knows of any strange stories here.

Luis points over to the big stone building across the way, a giant edifice that looks like it could be a mansion or an office building.

"That's the Antonino Mausoleum," he says. "Antonino was a senator during the Marcos martial law years. He died in a plane crash."

"The place is so big," I say. "How many people are buried there?"

"I think it is just three people," he says.

"Are you the caretaker there," I ask him.

"No, there hasn't been a caretaker there for something like ten years. Back in the mid-80's I had a friend who was hired by the family to be the caretaker there. The arrangement was that he was supposed to sleep inside the mausoleum every night. But every night he cannot sleep."

"How did you know this?" I ask him. "Did you go there too?"

"No, he used to come and tell me every day. He was always very nervous. He said every night at around midnight he heard a loud noise down in the basement. Like somebody pulling a big metal chain.

"Did he go check it out?"

"No he was too scared. Then he told me he used to see a body sitting at the dining table without a head.

This happened almost every night."

"So what did he do?"

"He worked there for nearly a year," he says. "Then he was found dead inside the mausoleum at the bottom of the stairs. He was found after several days. It was said that he slipped and fell down the stairs."

"What do you think happened?"

"I don't know," he says looking over at the mausoleum. "You know Senator Antonino died in a plane crash. Perhaps there were many body parts missing and they never found the head. Maybe that explains the headless body at the dining table. Maybe he is not resting in peace in that mausoleum. I cannot tell you. But up until now they cannot find anyone to be the caretaker there. Even the roving guard at the cemetery doesn't want to pass by there at night. He is afraid of going near the place. Me? I don't go there either." He pauses, looks down and starts to pick at the grass.

"Are there a lot of stories like that here," I ask, breaking the silence.

"In this area, not so many. But over there in the other section there are a lot of strange stories." He smiles and then stands up. "I have to go now. Nice to talk to you."

"Same here," I say. He picks up his clippers and shuffles over and begins trimming a nearby grave. I decide to take the short walk over the bridge to the "other section" Luis mentioned. When I get there I see various families preparing gravesites. Several caretakers manicure the grass. The rich colors of dusk have settled over the park. A strangely perfect setting and I decide not to ask any more questions.

***

Several nights later, at the beginning of the All Souls Day weekend, I walk in to Manila Memorial park and am greeted by a carnival-like atmosphere. There cannot be too many places on earth where people literally hold family parties on top of the graves of their dead relatives. Maybe it's no big deal to Filipinos, because that's just the way it is, and Filipinos do not think of a party-like atmosphere in the cemetery as anything unique. But any outsider would definitely say it is, well, different.

Where I come from, the United States, cemeteries are so solemn as to be practically morbid. People spend as little time as possible there and enjoying oneself inside a cemetery is a serious no-no.

When I first came to the Philippines several years ago and heard about this unique Filipino custom of honoring the dead by eating, drinking and singing on and around their graves once a year, the thought practically sickened me. And confused me. I knew Filipinos were highly religious. So why would they act like this inside a cemetery?

Well, I've come around. In fact it now makes more sense than the custom of a cemetery being such a morbid place. My take on it is if I were dead, I would not want to see my family come around once a year and be all sad and down. That would make my soul angry and restless. I'd want them to enjoy themselves and do the things we all did together when I was alive. That would make my spirit feel alive.

But still, to be honest, while it makes sense, it's an event that defies description. As I entered the park, my mind was playing tricks on me with everything I saw...

A giant, brightly lit, yellow and red Andok's roasted chicken sign towers over the landscape. Underneath the colorful sign young workers in yellow shorts and red aprons attend to the rotating dead chickens. In the Philippines, that smoke billowing off the hot coals represents succulent food. In India that smoke billowing off the hot coals means they are cremating a dead body. The world is definitely made up of different kinds of people with different approaches to things!

I spot a Burger Machine truck, a Shakey's Pizza booth and then somebody sticks a piece of paper in front of my face. What's this? A flyer selling a new subdivision in Laguna.

"Selling real estate in a cemetery?" I say astonished to the guy with the flyers.

"Just a job sir," he says smiling. Well, I think, if they can sell real estate why not take it to the limit. We walk past a Dunkin' Donuts banner and I imagine how next year all the vendors will be armed with bullhorns and mike systems to try to lure in the customers. "Folks, when visiting the dead, liven things up with Dunkin' Donuts. Sounds good, tastes even better!!"

Continuing to walk towards my father-in-law's grave, I spot a delivery driver from Chow King Chinese fast food race by on a motorcycle. Now this is one company which knows how to service its customers. Deliveries to the cemetery! I imagine that some guy was too lazy to get up and walk over to the Chow King stand that had been set up in the park, so he pulled out his cell phone and called up the local Chow King down the street. "Yes I'd like my order delivered to Manila Memorial Park, Eternal Gardens section, plot number 63. *Salamat po.*"

After we settle down at my father-in-law's grave, I soon decide to check out more of this extraordinary scene. The cemetery is mobbed with people spread out on nearly every inch of available grass. Howls of laughter fill the warm night air. People eat native foods. Teenagers sit around the colorfully lit fountain, as if it were any other Friday night of hangin' out. Little kids play tag, running roughshod over the graves of

people they do not even know. One family has some disco tunes blaring from a stereo and several teenagers have gotten up to dance. Another family has a stereo playing a tape of that all-time Filipino favorite ballad group, Michael Learns to Rock. What Filipino gathering would be complete without them?

People play mahjong and Scrabble—"that's d-e-a-d. Four points but triple word score, so that gives me 12 points. Your turn." It is as if All Souls Day is a good excuse to get some fresh air, sit on the grass and camp out for the night.

Pizza Hut and Shakey's Pizza have set up right next to each other and they are trying to see who can outdo the other. It is Friday night and the Philippine Basketball Association game is on. At the Pizza Hut booth, they're blasting a radio broadcast of the game on giant stereo speakers. When I walk over, the manager, Ariel, has just turned up the volume to the point where you have to shout to be heard. Nearly yelling, I ask him about the carnival atmosphere.

"It wasn't always like this," he says loudly with a big smile on his face. "Even five years ago it was different. It was more peaceful and solemn. Now it's very commercial. Like you said, it's like a carnival." But he is not criticizing it. He just laughs. When I say good-bye, he goes back to fiddling with the stereo, hoping to lure more customers.

But he is up against some serious competition. The Shakey's right next door has a TV and it is tuned to the PBA game. The volume has been turned up loud as well. A handful of potential customers stand around watching the game.

"It's a healthy competition," says the Shakey's manager when I inquire about all the noise and the party-like atmosphere. Back with my wife's family we sit around the candle-adorned grave and scarf *adobo* and *pinakbet*. The guys drink brandy while the women sip Bailey's. The kids run around the grass and play with abandon. Except for the fact that occasionally someone gets up and cleans the grave or lights another candle, it seems like any other family gathering.

"Why do Filipinos seem so happy here in a cemetery," I wonder aloud to whomever is listening. I know my take on it, but I want a Filipino to explain it to me. "Is it because being around all these dead people reminds them to enjoy life now?"

"No, they're happy because of the inheritance they received," my wife quips. This sends everybody in to hysterics. They forget my query but later I press my brother-in-law and he offers me this.

"If it was solemn," he says, "nobody would stay. The kids would be fighting with the parents. They'd be crying, 'We're bored, we want to go home!' But this way, we're still here. You say your prayers, you clean the grave. Anyway it's the dead's day. We're here with them." And that, of course, is what the unique celebra.... I mean observance, of All Souls Day in the Philippines is all about.

DOM'S BIG WEEKEND

Just call him DOM. It stands for Dirty Old Man. And this is his story, Halloween weekend, 1998.

First the get-up. Dom's outfit is everything and more that a dirty old man should be. So realistic it elicits reactions of fear, disgust and utter, deep down laughter from nearly everyone who lays their eyes on it. Dom has a serious bubble butt, a heavy midsection paunch, wears cheap white and blue pinstripe bell bottoms pulled up high over the huge paunch, a shabby black sport coat that barely fits, a dirty looking, white button down polo shirt—complemented for Halloween with a loosened black tie imprinted with dancing white skeletons—a long, gaudy silk scarf with colorful fish imprinted on it wrapped around his neck, a baseball cap worn sideways on his head and a big green, round earring hanging from his left earlobe (Dom is definitely not gay).

Then, of course, there's the face. A full head mask so realistic, people who see it have trouble distinguishing if Dom is a real guy or not. Dom has a severely wrinkled face, bald top with scraggly blond hair spraying wildly out from the sides and back, bulbous pockmarked nose and the few teeth remaining growing out in every direction.

The icing on the cake is Dom the character and personality. He walks hunched over but with a purpose, holding a rolled up umbrella in one hand that he uses as his cane. In the other hand he carries a ladies' thong panty. When he sees a woman, he has a heart attack right on the spot, grasping his heart and stumbling backwards. He approaches men and women and holds up the thong panty and takes a whiff of the panty. Often times he stands in front of a group of people, especially those who look like they are taking themselves way too seriously, and sticks a finger in his big rubber nose, then wipes the imaginary boogie on the table cloth right next to their pasta.

Depending on the person who sees him, Dom is disgusting and endearing. Those who are loose love Dom. Those who are wound tighter than a spool of thread hate him. Dom loves them all for Halloween is Dom's time out. He goes all out sparing no passersby from his schtick. Dom knows in a world so straight most of the year, he's only allowed out to do his thing on Halloween. He takes full advantage of the opportunity.

Dom's Halloween weekend begins on Friday night, October 30th, in Manila's fashionable business district of Makati, where many of the beautiful people of the Philippines gather regularly. As Dom stumbles up the path of the Hotel Intercontinental, the boys in the parking lot burst out laughing.

The guys at the front door of the Intercon also laugh when they see Dom and allow him into the lobby. Dom's destination is the Euphoria disco, but he lingers in the lobby for ten minutes greeting the hotel guests. Dom takes a load off and sits in a big comfortable chair in the lobby, occasionally picking his bulbous rubber nose. He waves to the people leaving and entering the hotel and those just walking through the lobby. Dom gets a few waves back and several smiles. Surprisingly though, most just walk by and feign no reaction. They look and keep on walking. But Dom knows better. A look of no reaction is a reaction. Unlike Dom, real people don't mask their emotions very well. Many want to laugh but they cannot. Several look borderline angry. They have been caught acting too serious. Some can take it and laugh, while others can't take it and pretend not to have seen a thing. Dom strikes again.

Dom stumbles over to the Euphoria disco. At the front counter he encounters two young, ultra hot, Filipina chicks standing against the wall. Their hair is done to perfection, the makeup thick and heavy, the outfits fashionable and tight. Dom approaches the ladies and immediately grasps his heart and stumbles backwards, as if he's having a heart attack. He then holds up the lace thong panty and takes a whiff. He offers them a whiff. The look on the two girls' faces is priceless; complete and utter contempt and disgust. They seem to be asking the question, "Who is this slovenly pig?" But of course they can do nothing about it because it's Halloween.

Dom has a huge laugh at their expense, as does the staff of Euphoria. Dom further humors himself by thinking of the obvious; underneath that dirty old man could stand Leonardo Di Caprio. However, the two airheads looking for Mr. Pretty Boy cannot think that deeply. All they see is a real live dirty old man. And they hate him with a passion. Dom strikes again.

Dom stumbles down the stairs into the disco. This was the place three years ago on Halloween where he took the first prize of P10,000 in the costume contest. Apparently Euphoria's slipped more than a tad since then. Tonight is their Halloween party and the prizes are lame. A couple of overnight stays in Subic Bay and several P500 gift certificates. Oh well, that's not going to stop Dom from enjoying himself.

The disco is barely half full and Dom notices that the crowd on hand has all come in rather strange costumes tonight; each and everyone is dressed as a yuppie. It takes him a minute to realize that the yuppie get-up is what these people wear everyday.

Dom mingles amongst the crowd, personally greeting everyone he sees. Especially the ladies. Some scurry in fear at the sight of Dom. Others break down in laughter, especially when he holds up the panty or when he picks his nose and wipes the fake boogie on the shirt of someone who's not looking. The smiles on some of the ladies' faces impresses Dom. Clearly, a sector of the female population has a soft heart for a dirty old man.

Come contest time, Dom walks away with first prize. Except this is no big deal as his only competition is a gay with his body painted gold and a basket of fruit on top of his head, and a guy in jeans wearing a skeleton mask.

Then Dom is presented with his prize; a P500 gift certificate, two cans of warm Budweiser and a bright red Budweiser cap. The overnights in Subic are given out in a raffle draw and are claimed by several of the yuppies. Dom complains to the manager, but she says, "That's just the way we do it here." Dom wants to strangle her with his panty, but decides to stumble out instead.

Dom walks through the lobby of the Intercon and the bellman opens the door.

"I won first prize tonight," Dom tells the bellman. The bellman laughs and says, "Yes sir, what did you win?" Dom stops. "I won two round trip tickets to Bicutan. Three days, two nights at the Bicutan Hilton, round trip transfers via deluxe pedicab, and a free tour of the famous squatter colony and wet market on the railroad tracks." All the boys working the front burst out laughing.

It's past one in the morning but Dom is feeling a little under appreciated. He wants some more action.

Several blocks away Dom finds a bar called Venezia. Several BMW's, a Mercedes and a Jaguar are parked outside. Dom walks into the crowded bar and all heads immediately turn to gawk. Dom gawks back and gets confused. Everyone looks exactly the same; pretty, clean cut, same clothes, same face.

Dom makes the rounds, performing his schtick for the crowd. Some of the people laugh, others get that look of contempt, especially the guys whose ladies get propositioned by Dom. Dom decides it's better to leave than stay and have a drink.

Saturday night, October 31st, Halloween, Dom returns to the land of the pretty people and shuffles his way into the Hard Rock Café. The Hard Rock's giving away two round trip tickets to Las Vegas tonight. Dom wants those tickets as he knows dirty old men are well appreciated in Las Vegas.

Dom immediately finds himself amongst a much more hospitable crowd than the previous night. The Hard Rock is packed and over a hundred people have come in costume. Amongst the more memorable get-ups is a man with his head coming out of his chest, several indescribable monsters that have no particular name but are, nonetheless, well conceived, a man painted in blue and covered with writhing snakes, a bloodied mangled looking guy with one eye down by his cheek, his arm cut in half and an axe sticking out of his back and various other crazies who have spared nothing in celebrating Halloween.

Another thing that makes Dom smile is the amount of children on hand at the Hard Rock. Many have come dressed to the nines for Halloween and they are all having a good time. Many of the kids have fun with Dom as they pinch his big bubble butt and squeeze his big rubber nose. Dom returns the favor and offers to let them fondle the panty. None takes him up on the offer, however.

Dom works the huge crowd, greeting everyone whom he walks past, especially the ones who did not dress up tonight. The sick bastard has them rolling in the aisles. One foreigner grabs Dom's panty and puts it on his head. When Dom picks his nose and wipes it on the man's shirt, the man decides to hand back the panty. At another table Dom offers to shake a man's hand. When the man sticks out his hand, Dom pulls his own hand back and scratches his head.

But, of course, Dom is really more interested in the ladies. Many cringe in fear when the ugly old man saunters up to them. The face repulses them, the bubble butt grosses them out, the nose picking disgusts them, the panty shocks them. Interestingly most, in time, soften up to the old low life. Dom actually gets propositioned by several ladies who cannot seem to resist his charm. One seriously asks for his phone number. Another wants to meet him somewhere after the gig. Dom is mightily impressed and tells himself that's why he loves Halloween. For this day has shown him that there truly are many women out there who really do have a thing for an endearing, dirty old man.

It's not until sometime past one in the morning that they whittle the contest down to the ten finalists. Dom makes it! But he and all the other contestants have had to endure a marathon evening, thanks to the Hard Rock management who are milking the characters for all that they are worth. When the judges mercifully hand in their final votes, Dom loses out. The winner is the man with his head boring out of his chest. A deserved winner, no doubt, and he happily takes his two round trip tickets to Vegas. Oh yeh, and after handing him the two tickets, the Hard Rock gifts the guy with all of P5,000 spending money for his stay in Vegas. Sounds like a trick, not a treat.

As for Dom, as a finalist he leaves with more nick nacks to add to his collection from the previous night; a Lucky Strike ash tray, a silvery Power Page back pack, and a P1,000 gift certificate to the Hard Rock Café. Sort of hollow on Halloween, but what the heck. Anyway, Dom still feels satisfied, for he knows it was more than just his costume that messed with the minds of so many people. It was his personality; sick, funny, endearing and disgusting. All together it was enough to get nasty looks from the tightly wound, laughter from the gut from those who are loose and even propositions from several ladies who bought into the whole schtick. Above all, Dom's weekend brought forth the essential question that Halloween poses each year; and that is: "Who's really normal around here and who's really abnormal?" It's a rhetorical question and Dom, happy at already knowing the answer, shuffles off into the night.

"Come on Joe," he always says, "tonight you try balut."

"Balut?" I yell back. "I don't eat duck abortions!"

A NIGHT AT THE COCKFIGHTS

Of course, it's all about the money. Of that there can be no question. Money is why nearly 1,500 people, all but four of them men, are out at the smoke-filled Elorde cockpit in Sucat, Parañaque, Metro Manila on a Monday night. Money is why many will stay until the deep hours of the night. And money is why many will finally leave at the finish close to dawn.

Oh sure, the color of the cockfights, or *sabong* as it is often called, is as good as it gets, especially to a foreigner like myself. The cockfights offer that rare combination of spectacle, tradition and pure violence that one can only find in a few places on earth, maybe the bullfights in Spain, and Muay Thai boxing in Thailand.

But perhaps only in the Philippines is the spectacle as blatantly out front and in your face; the hard scrabble men legally gambling thousands of pesos on two birds with razor sharp knives tied to their legs and fighting to the death inside a glass walled dirt pit; the impossibly loud, primeval sound as hundreds of *cristos*—bet takers—rise to their feet before each match and shout the bets of their financiers into the air, flashing their incredibly complicated hand signals while looking for someone in the arena who will take their wager; the fact that many of these cristos do this for a living, with many putting kids through school via their earnings here; the fast moving action as each deadly match takes only a few minutes.

Then there's the notion that while cockfighting may be a blood sport, it is unquestionably a gentleman's game. There's no rule book and no house to bet with. All bets are made with other bettors and on an honor system. Nothing is written down. After each match, everyone pays up. When the loser is too far away to hand over the money, he rolls up the cash into a little ball and throws it across the arena to the winner. Even if the money gets dropped under the bleachers, nobody steals it. On the rare occasion that some joker tries to run without paying, payment will be extracted by a quickly formed mob, and it will not be painless.

And yes, there's even compassion for the cocks. Monday nights are derby nights at Elorde. Cock owners bring their best cocks to fight for big prize money, which tonight will be P100,000 to the winning handler. If the bird loses and dies, he will not get eaten, like at an ordinary cockfight.

"Some guys will bury their cocks after it is killed," says Johnny Elorde, who runs the Elorde cockpit. "The cock may have brought him good fortune."

And, yes, fortune is what this ritual is all about. After an hour of watching, I realize atmosphere can only take me so far. Although not a regular gambler, I decide to place a bet.

Another cockfight is getting set to begin. The two handlers bring their cocks into the pit. The pit consists of a hard packed dirt floor raised up to eye level and completely surrounded by glass. Bleachers rise up on all four sides. The handlers stand under lighted signs hanging over the middle of the pit. One sign says 'meron,' which literally means 'to have.' The other sign says 'wala,' which means 'have nothing.'

Each handler is joined by another handler whose cock will fight in the following bout. The purpose of the extra cock is to help each cock in the current bout

warm up. The idea is to get the cocks angry, which any fighting cock will instinctively do when face to face with another male. Each handler holds his fighting cock by the tail and faces him towards the extra cock. Both birds try to attack each other, but are held back by their handlers.

As this is going on, a man holding a microphone, the *llamadore*, walks around inside the pit looking into the audience. He is looking for somebody who wants to put up P12,000. The respective handlers bet against each other and sometimes one handler puts up more money than the other. They need to even the bet and finally he finds a taker.

As soon as the bet between the handlers is even, the cristos rise up and begin their ritual shouting. The two extra cocks leave and the two remaining handlers face their cocks against each other. The hot and sweaty arena immediately explodes in a cacophony of throaty noise as the cristos bark into the air, looking for someone to take their bets. It is a deafening noise, a frothy and guttural sound that seems to come from the depths of the crowd's very soul, something akin to the days at the Roman Coliseum when the Romans fed the Christians to the lions.

Amidst this spine tingling tumult, I flag down an Elorde cristo, a guy named Hermil, who is standing a few seats away. Bets are taken by hand signals—fingers flashed to the side mean hundreds, fingers flashed pointing down mean thousands. I flash him two fingers to the side and give a pulling motion with my hands. He turns around, looks up into the bleachers and shouts into the noisy bedlam. With one hand he loosely covers his mouth—so as not to spit on anyone sitting nearby—while at the same time repeatedly shouting 'Meron!' With the other hand he holds two fingers to the side. I notice he catches the attention of another cristo in the bleachers and they exchange several hand signals. Hermil turns around towards me and indicates the bet is in. I have P200 on 'Meron,' the favorite.

Inside the pit each handler removes the leather cover from the razor sharp blade anchored on the cock's leg. The *sententiador* (referee) carefully wipes each blade with a rag, assuring no foreign substances alter the fight. The handlers bring the cocks to the center of the ring where the cocks peck at each other. The handlers step back and drop their cocks onto the dirt. The crowd settles down to watch and the fight begins.

Meron does not waste any time and immediately attacks Wala. Meron jumps and kicks and mauls his opponent. Within seconds Wala is laying on the dirt floor writhing in pain while blood spills from his wounds. Moments later he is dead.

Hermil turns towards the bleachers and collects my winnings from the other cristo, who folds up the bills and tosses them down. Hermil then hands me the money. I have no feeling for the dead bird as it feels good to win.

After the handlers leave the ring, a man holding a broom and dust pan climbs in and sweeps up the loose feathers. Within moments the ritual begins anew. A new set of cocks enters the ring, the llamadore helps even the bet of the handlers, the cristos then rise up in mass and the arena erupts in absolute bedlam.

For the next match I up the bet to P300. Some people choose a cock because he is the bigger of the two, or they know the handler has a good bloodline. I choose the underdog, 'Wala,' for no other reason than I like his color, a sharp mixture of white, rust and brown. I flash Hermil three fingers to the side and wave towards Wala. He quickly finds a taker, again in the bleachers. This match takes a few minutes but I win again. Meron put up a good fight but he ran out of gas and slowly fell over and died from his wounds.

At this point I'm feeling like a genius and that this could be my big night. This kind of attitude, of course, is the biggest mistake a gambler can make. As quick as I was up P500, I am soon down P600, having lost four matches in a row. My confidence is now shot. No big deal, I think. Just the breaks of the game. I decide to take a breather and have a look around. It's now one in the morning.

I walk out of the arena and a man grabs my arm.

"Come," he says waving his hand, "you see cock doctor." He leads the way under the wooden bleachers. As we walk I notice the air smells like chicken liver. We walk past the credit window and into the corner under the bleachers, where several people stand gathered.

It is a scene of pure carnage. This is where the doctors have set up a makeshift bird hospital. The hospital consists of a knee high table and two plastic chairs. One doctor is asleep in his chair while the other works feverishly on an injured cock. More out of a desire to finish the job, it appears, rather than to save a life.

On the floor sits a small card board box overflowing with bloodied rooster legs. Several smiling young guys see me eyeing the box. One of them is holding his mangled bird in his hands. The cock is still alive but has countless nasty red gashes and is missing a leg. I ask him if the bird will live. He shakes his head and says the doctor just looked over the cock and cannot do anything.

"Come on Joe," he says as he holds up the cock, "we eat *pulutan* (drinking snacks) and drink beer." We all laugh.

The doctor continues to work on the current patient. His lap is covered by a thick rubber mat, and on the mat he holds the bloodied bird, who sits motionless. He works under a glaring lamp. His bare hands are almost completely red with blood. Feathers lay scattered all over the floor. The doctor lifts up the bird's wing and feathers, looking for wounds. There looks to be dozens of bloody gashes.

When the doctor finds a wound, he quickly rips out the surrounding feathers. Then, using tweezers, he sticks cotton deep inside the gash, blots the blood, then pulls out the cotton. Occasionally the bird writhes in pain. Then the doctor pours a white anti-biotic powder on the wound.

"That's Aji-no-moto," says an onlooker, referring to the white powdered flavor enhancer used for cooking. The handful of guys standing around laugh. The doctor then stitches the wound and quickly moves on to the next cut. It takes him twenty minutes to repair this bird.

"He won't fight again for a year and a half," says the man who led me back here.

Next to the makeshift bird hospital sit the cock houses. The cock houses are sectioned-off plywood rooms where the owners stay with their roosters. Some of the cocks here will be engaged in a fight to the death within the hour. Others have recently returned from the dirt pit and lie belly up dead on the floor. Occasionally a live cock hollers a loud, shrilly crow into the air.

In one room, two guys in their twenties from Laguna, a town just outside of the metropolis, keep watch over their cock, who paces the floor. The bird looks big and strong.

"I will bet P22,000 on my bird," the one man says with a shy smile. The opponent will be the bird in the next cock house. I walk over and look in the door. There a big black fighting cock stands proudly under a green metal cage with a lone bare bulb glaring down from the top. The bird looks like a monster. His owner, also a man in his twenties, just stands quietly looking over the cock.

The man looks to be meditating or praying.

I walk to the front of the arena and wander inside the *gaffer* room, which sits opposite the ticket booth and the entrance gate. The gaffer room is a bright, bare bones area where the birds come to have the steel blades attached to their left leg. The gaffer room is also where the cocks come to get weighed.

Dong is 26 years old and has been a gaffer for 10 years. Like all gaffers he carries a small kit, inside of which sit the tools of his trade: razor sharp steel blades, leather blade covers, a sharpening stone, thread and tape. He says the kit cost him P15,000.

A gaffer works for the cock owner and gets paid only if the owner wins money. Tonight Dong is gaffing for the men from Laguna whom I just talked with in the cock house. The owner holds the bird while Dong carefully performs his job.

First he meticulously wraps tape around the left leg of the cock. Then he places a crutch inside the tape. He then selects a blade from the kit. He carefully sharpens the blade on the sharpening stone, testing it on his fingernail for sharpness. Once he's satisfied, he places the blade in the crutch and secures it with string. He eyes the blade, making sure it sticks straight backwards. Once on, he places a leather cover over the blade and fastens it with more string. The cock is now ready for the fight.

Several minutes later the cocks enter the ring carried by their owners. The *sabong* ritual begins with the cristos rising in mass and shouting out for bets. The arena quickly becomes engulfed in that incredibly loud, bone chilling roar.

I figure I'll give it one more shot to try to get back. The favorite, Meron, is the big black fighting cock whose owner looked to be meditating in the cock house. I waver, having little confidence. Amidst the tumult I find

Hermil the cristo, and flash three fingers to the side and indicate Meron. A minute later he turns to me and flashes me hand signals to show there are odds. My bet is P375 to win P300.

I stand on the ground with my face nearly pressed up against the glass of the pit, at eye level with the cocks. Suddenly, something catches my eye. A waiter delivers a plate of fried chicken to a man sitting several rows up. The irony of this act does not escape me and I laugh to myself. As the fight begins, Wala, the cock from Laguna, comes out firing. He jumps, he pecks, and he stomps. He has Meron down and injured. It looks like it'll be over in a matter of seconds. I'm quickly resigned to being out P1,000 for the night.

Meron is injured and lays on the dirt unable to stand up. Wala, however, cannot finish him off as he is exhausted and slowing down. Repeatedly the sententiador picks up the two birds by the back of the neck and brings their heads together. As long as both cocks peck each other, the fight will continue. Even though he looks dead, my rooster, Meron, keeps pecking.

. It goes on like this for nine minutes. Early on the crowd had quieted down and simply watched the match. However, there's a ten minute time limit to each match and the Meron folks are starting to get excited as they sense escaping with a draw. As the clock ticks to the final minute, the noise in the arena rises. I stand on the floor pounding on the glass.

Then with 30 seconds left the sententiador again picks up the birds. My cock, Meron, pecks, but Wala, even though he's still standing, doesn't. The judge tries two more times with the same result. The arena erupts as incredibly, miraculously, Meron has come back from the dead and is declared the winner.

And indeed I feel as if I am back from the dead as well. Instead of being down P1,000, I'm only down P300. My heart is pounding and suddenly the juice has returned. I collect my P300 from Hermil, give him a high five and take my seat in the stands.

By the time the derby ends, it's five o'clock in the morning and I' m back up P300. Before I leave, I slip Hermil P30, the standard 10% of the winnings.

Outside I notice the faint light of dawn in the sky over Manila Memorial Park, a cemetery right across the street. Several people stand on Sucat Road, waiting for a jeepney to pick them up and take them to school or work.

I walk to the road and I can feel the excitement coursing through my veins, as if I've been struck by a bolt of electricity. And as I wait for a taxi to pick me up and take me home, I think of the simple yet philosophical words of Johnny Elorde, who likes to remind those who are down, that the beauty of *sabong* is that you're never far from redemption.

"Don't worry," he says laughing, "In the cockfights you must remember, there's always another fight."

THE TOWN CRIER

He cruises the dark streets during the deepest hours of the night. Slung over his forearm are his "little bundles of joy," which are attentively placed inside a wicker basket, and kept warm with a carefully wrapped blanket. Sometimes you see him, but most of the time you just hear him, shouting into the night, his forlorn wail piercing the still of the darkness, arousing the restless and the hungry, probing the sleep of everyone in the neighborhood, especially the young, who surely must grow up with that haunting cry emblazoned in their slumbering subconscious.

"Baluuuuuuuuuut!!" Out of the distance comes the drawn-out, faint cry, the sing-song call of a warm voice in the night. And then several seconds later yet another, louder "Baluuuuuuuuut!," a timeless sound, one that has filled the warm, tropical nights for a thousand years, without letup to this day. If the "Town Crier" still exists, he lives in the Philippines and he is known as the Balut Man.

I have always thought balut, and thus the balut man, to be a very mysterious part of Filipino culture. Since I came to the Philippines in the early 90's, balut has always seemed like the strangest food in the whole world. I love boiled eggs. But the idea of peeling an egg shell and biting into a dead, aborted duck has not exactly been on my list of culinary delights.

"But it's good for the knees," everyone says, meaning

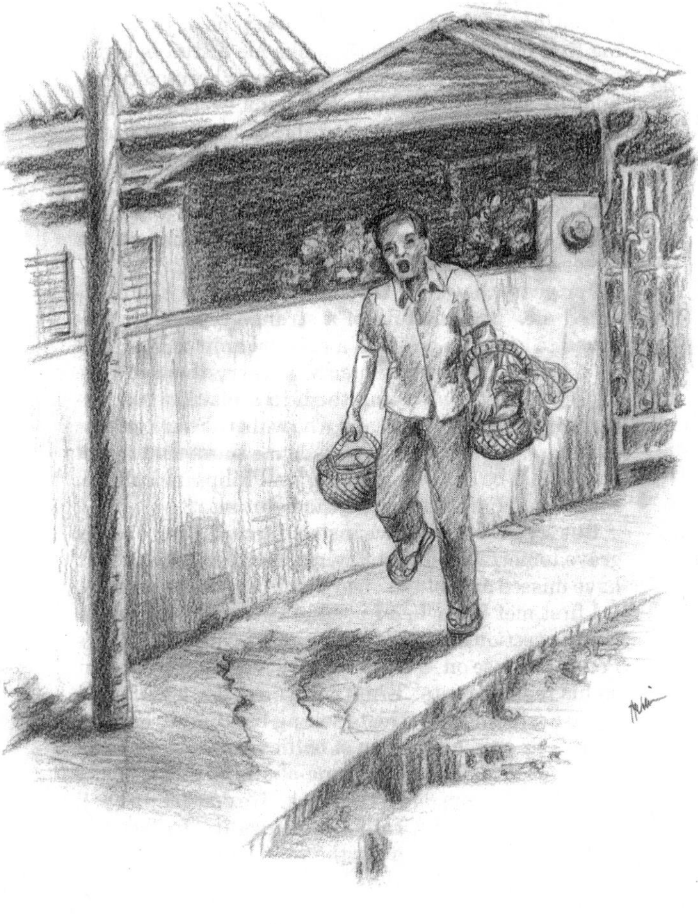

that balut will somehow make me a stud in bed.

"Hmmm," I ponder. "Sexual powers heretofore unknown? Maybe I should try this balut everyone's talking about." But I haven't been able to get up the nerve. I've always declined the offer of a balut, even turning my eyes when I see other people peeling the shell and sucking out that poor bird who never had a chance. Besides, I have never quite understood what strong knees and sex have in common.

For years, however, the concept of balut has fascinated me. The mixture of a strange type of egg believed to have the power of a magical aphrodisiac, and sold mainly at night by men who carry them in cute wicker baskets, wrapping them in a blanket like babies to keep them warm, and who walk the dark streets howling into the night, has made me think that to sell balut must be a special calling in Philippine culture. I wonder if Filipinos revere the balut man?

But try balut? Well I've insisted that if I went to my grave tomorrow without having tasted one, I wouldn't have missed anything. Then I met Boy, the balut man.

I first met Boy when I used to stay regularly in the Ermita section of Manila. Boy always walks by Tadel's Pension House on Arquiza Street several times a night on his regular route. Ermita is a busy place with a lot of guys walking the streets selling balut and you tend to hear as good a selection of balut vendors as one can imagine. Boy's balut call is one-of-a-kind and is easily recognizable from down the block. He doesn't just yell the word balut, but, rather, he sings it. In fact I've noticed he doesn't even say the word balut. If I were to spell it for you it would look something like this:

"Haaloooooooahh!!" It is a long, drawn-out and loud cry, leaping forth from the depth of his soul. Boy is the Pavarotti of balut vendors.

From my second floor room I could always hear him clearly and when I did, I bought *penoy* from him. Penoy is more up my alley as it's the same as a boiled chicken egg except it comes from a duck. I rather like penoy because it has a richer taste and texture.

Besides Boy's great balut call, I like to buy from Boy because he's a great guy. He's always so upbeat and so into selling balut. He promotes it and gets excited about it.

"Come on Joe," he always says, "tonight you try balut."

"Balut?" I yell back. "I don't eat duck abortions!" Boy gets a laugh out of that line. One night as I sat on the steps peeling the shell off my penoy, Boy put his basket down and lit up a cigarette. I had a chance to ask him about himself.

He said he was 47 years old (he looked 35) and has been selling balut since 1974, always in the Ermita area. He starts the night with 60 balut and 15 penoy, which he buys daily from a middleman who gets them from the province of Bulacan. He starts at two in the afternoon and finishes at midnight, or until his basket is nearly empty. He works Monday through Friday and lives in Tondo during the week. On the weekends he takes a bus to Nueva Ecija, where his wife and ten year old daughter live. I never asked Boy how much he makes because, well, I knew it wasn't a lot. At the time, he was selling balut for six pesos. It doesn't take a math whiz to realize he's living from day to day.

"It's a job for a poor man like me," Boy said with his characteristic smile.

"How many times in a night do you yell, 'baluuuut'?" I asked.

"Ohhh, many times!"

"Well, how about from the corner of Mabini St. to the corner of M. H. del Pilar. One block."

"Ten times," he said.

"Let me hear your style. I know you're good at it."

"Haaloooooooooahh!!," he wailed. Like a sergeant calling his troops to attention.

"You don't say 'balut!!?'"

"No," and he cried out again, "haaloooooooahh!!!" loud enough for all Ermita to hear.

"You have the best balut call in Ermita," I said. "It's different."

"Well, I have to call you, right? You don't know I'm here. Maybe you are sleeping."

"That's true," I said. "I came from my room when I heard you."

"See. You heard me. I have many customers like that. They are sleeping when I come to the door and I shout 'Haaloooooooahh!!' They wake up and buy two balut. Every night."

"How come the balut man always works at night," I asked.

"Because people make boom-boom at night," he answered.

"You know I've never eaten a balut. I only eat penoy."

"But it's good!!," he said excitedly. "You eat one now Joe." Then he pulled a balut out of his basket.

"No way, I'm scared. I don't like the face of the poor duck. He's looking right at you, it's so disgusting."

"If you don't like the face, then eat it in the dark."

"Well what about the feathers and the beak that crunches when you eat it?"

"Nooo!! It's good for you. Make you good at boom-boom. And it's good for the knees. Make you strong at night time. Come on, here."

"Get out of here," I joked. "I don't believe you. Good for boom-boom?"

"Yes, really!!"

"I don't understand," I said, obviously stalling. "What do the knees have to do with making boom-boom?"

"Make you strong Joe. That guy over there just ate four balut."

"He must have his girlfriend with him tonight," I said. Boy laughed.

"Yes he does," Boy said. "He has girlfriend tonight. So now you eat balut?" Boy was insistent tonight. He cracked the tip of the shell on the sidewalk and handed me the balut. By now a handful of people had gathered around to watch. It felt like an initiation. I peeled off the top part of the shell, but didn't look. I knew I was at the point of no-return.

"First you eat soup," Boy said. We counted off together, one, two and three and I sucked down the juice. To be honest, it tasted pretty good. As I swallowed I nodded my approval.

"See?" Boy said. "Good ahh?" But now came the hard part. And I figured it best not to waste any time. Boy led me on. We counted together. "One, two and three...."

I gulped it down in one bite. It went down pretty smooth. No beak. No hair. No beady eyes. After five years of denial at least now I could say I had finally eaten balut. I felt like I'd been let in on a special Filipino secret.

With everyone laughing, Boy picked up his basket and said with a big smile, "Hey Joe, balut good ahh? Now you are Filipino." I handed him ten pesos and told him to keep the change. Then he was off. In a few moments I heard his cry fill the night.

SOUNDS IN THE DARKNESS

A warm, soft breeze passes through the open screened window, gently nudging the curtains, which slowly sway back and forth. Darkness has filled this quiet room, but outside the sky still has traces of light. The rich and deep colors lay scattered in all parts of the sky—orange, deep blue, brown, green, red—as if some impulsive artist slipped on a blindfold, and went wild with his brush and palette. The artist must still be at work for the colors seem to get stronger by the second. Then quickly, though, his painting gets engulfed by the oncoming darkness. Night has descended upon Manila.

Actually, it is early evening in the metropolis. No longer day, not quite night. I have been spared this day from the tumult that surely rages at this time—the hordes spilling out of the sprawling and towering concrete and glass high rises and onto the crowded streets, jostling and fighting for a little space, trying to move forward, no matter how small a distance, just anything so they can keep moving, so they can get home.

Instead I am sitting in the newly arrived darkness surrounded by silence. It is my space, my little corner of the world. And it is comfortable. A rare treat in this hectic town.

In the distance I can hear the soft hum of this teeming city. It's a steady but far away buzz. When I listen closely to the buzz, I realize I can actually feel it. It

dawns on me that the ground is vibrating. Not surprising considering the explosion of life this city harbors.

But while the city still radiates, it is also changing.
Early evening is that time of day when the transition
to a different time—night time—begins. It is a time
when the heat of the day begins to fade, but still lays
quite heavy. It is a time when people, animals and
things begin to slow down, but surely there is still
plenty of action.

The quiet of this early evening allows me to hear the
sounds coming from the village in which I am sitting
and the city in the far distance. For some reason the
sounds are much more difficult to hear during the daylight hours. Under day time skies, sounds become dif-
fused and escape. Under the cloak of darkness, sounds
hang around and become amplified.

The sounds are familiar to one and all who live here,
but hardly ever noticed. Somewhere out there I hear
the faint roar of a jeepney driving away. In my mind I
can see the silvery metallic machine spewing a plume
of gritty black poison into the hot and moist air, as
people standing nearby on the side of the road cover
their faces. I picture the jeepney then disappearing into
the fray, to be replaced soon by another and another
and another in an endless parade of colorful, cheap,
noisy and poison spitting transportation.

Then comes the sound of the chimes. "Ba, bah, bahh,
bahhh!!. Four bells rising from low to high. It is the
sound of the cadence chimes which indicate that an announcement that nobody will understand is forthcom-
ing. The chimes blare from the old megaphone speakers
of the Uniwide Warehouse Club store somewhere in the
near distance. The store is actually not very close, but
I sit downwind. The scratchy inaudible voice makes an
announcement. Thousands of people hear it but nobody
understands it. The quiet of the night soon returns.

The soft breeze continues to gently move the curtains and cool my perspiring skin. Outside my window, a dog starts to bark into the darkness. Within seconds another joins in and then soon another. The barking disease spreads and before long, dozens of dogs are carrying on. Over nothing, no doubt. After several minutes, they all tire and call it quits.

A group of kids scamper by, yelping and laughing. Early evening everywhere is the time kids wander the neighborhood. They run and gallop and soon they are out of range, their playful sounds disappearing with them.

The quiet soon becomes interrupted by a water delivery truck, which lumbers down the street, its wheels bouncing in and out of a pothole, making a loud clanking sound. When the truck has gone, the relaxing silence returns, still accompanied by that faint buzz of the far away city, now under darkness but still alive, still chaotic, still exploding in infinite different directions.

In the quiet I hear the tinkling sound of a spoon and fork scraping a plate. Something so simple and basic, yet essential. A spoon, a fork and a dish. The sound resonates, as if it's in stereo. It's coming from somewhere outside, and I imagine a slightly pudgy, shirtless guy sitting at a worn, wooden picnic table, under the tin sheeting, bent over a giant plate of rice with a small fried fish on the side, his mouth bulging and full, the fork in his left hand holding and separating the food, the spoon in his right hand continuing to scrape and shovel.

He eats and eats and eats some more, until finally ending it all in a crescendo of tinkling, the spoon and fork hitting the plate as he scrapes every last morsel of rice and fish and places it all into his mouth. When he's finished the silence returns.

The chimes come again and as usual they are followed by another incomprehensible announcement. A rooster shouts into the darkness. A gate to a house is slammed shut. A radio gets turned on and plays a Tagalog love song. It's one of those cheap little portable radios that makes the music sound like it's being broadcast from far away, perhaps Samar.

Like all the other sounds piercing the warm darkness, though, the radio does not erase nor dominate the silence. It's an accompaniment to the quiet, a compliment to the scene. Something like what wall paper is to a room. The song continues to come from somewhere out there, as does the faint but clear sound of another plume-spewing jeepney, as well as the other sounds, sounds of a wild, far off metropolis still raging, and a nearby village going through its daily routine.

As the gentle breeze continues to blow through my window, I sit in the quiet darkness of the early evening and I listen.

MOON OVER MANILA

Subtlety. This is the beauty of the moon. In its light, which is actually sunlight, only in a backhanded fashion, you can look at people without really looking at them. You can see the city without seeing everything. The blemishes, so easily revealed by the harsh light of the sun, are coyly hidden by the moon. The moon allows you to see at night, yet only what it wants you to see. The moon allows you to think. Its seductive powers awaken your mind at a time when the mind is normally at rest.

Our ancient friend, who has captivated and enraptured people since time began, has been up to his old tricks. As usual he started small, just a thin sliver, and nobody paid him any mind. But he was there, hovering over the city every night, growing bigger with each passing day, culminating in a glorious big, fat full moon. Nary a cloud bothered the moon, either, and for days he showed off like we haven't seen in a long time. He was practically shameless. Heck, his icy cool light even brought us some of the finest weather ever felt in this city.

When the moon was over Manila, you could see this city in ways that you never thought possible. If Manileños found themselves muttering quietly that their sprawling and teeming city actually, for once, looked pretty and, dare I say, charming, they needed not wonder about their sanity. If they found themselves the recipient of warm and serene feelings towards their fellow citizens, they needed not fret. They could just blame it on the moon and know that they were not alone. For the moon, hanging like a 200-watt bulb in the dark sky, cast its net far and wide, affecting people all over Manila, in ways subtle and mysterious.

For instance, the moon, round and silvery and lying on the horizon like a drunken Buddha, caught the eye of a Northwest Airlines pilot, who was five minutes away from landing at Ninoy Aquino International Airport. When he saw the moon he felt like flying right into it, if that were possible. Of course that was not possible. So he did the next best thing. Instead of coming straight in for a landing, he gave the passengers a thrilling fly-by of that big, flat glowing disc in the sky.

This only served to take the passengers away from their view of the city below, which, everyone silently agreed, looked positively enchanting bathed in the light of the full moon. And when the pilot brought the plane down to the ground, he landed as if on a giant bed of cotton, despite the bumpy runway at the Ninoy Aquino Airport. The pilot swore it was the best landing he ever performed.

Down at Manila Bay, the night light reflected brilliantly off the water and captured the boatman's attention. He cruised in his *banca*—ironically named Luna—out to one of the giant oil tankers anchored in the bay. Although he did not need the moon to manoeuver a route he had plied maybe a thousand times, this night the ride seemed easier and more pleasant.

On board Luna he carried a lady of the night, whose well washed and groomed body sparkled under the gaze of the moon. A Greek cargo ship had anchored in the bay that afternoon after having been at sea for over four months. No doubt it was the moon, blazing in the night sky like a white fireball, and whose light streaked through the cabin porthole, that led her to make love to the Greek seaman three times that night. For once it did not feel like a job. Afterwards, instead of dressing right away and cruising back to the shore with her newly bulging purse, she laid in the seaman's arms and stared out the porthole. Staring back was another man—the man in the moon—who gave her a mischievous wink.

When the moon was over Manila, its night time glare also shone in the eye of the President, who sat at his desk in his second floor office in Malacañan Palace. He had been working late, dutifully going through some papers of an important, but highly controversial bill he wanted passed. When he saw the moon staring at him through the bay window, though, he put down his pen for a moment and gazed at the bright rock in the sky and the city whose light it caressed.

"What a lovely place," he thought. A peaceful feeling filled him inside. The nation thanked the moon for that.

All over Manila, the moon cast its seductive net, bringing lots of people out of their houses. As usual, the streets were a traffic nightmare. Nobody seemed to mind, though. They were all captivated by the moon. People stared out their car windows at the fat, milky disc, while they went nowhere. Many even said to themselves, "It's lucky we're stuck in traffic, so we can look at the moon." Funny, you couldn't even hear horns blaring that night. That's how loud the moon was.

Taking advantage of the traffic quagmire and the moon's bewitching powers, the little girls selling *sampaguita* in the streets did a big business. Sampaguita made their way all over Manila, and the cool, breezy moonlit night was filled with the flowers' sweet fragrance.

This was especially so in the Luneta and Rizal

Park, which had become a positively magical place that night. All the couples and families strolling and lounging under the moon's guise bought the fragrant flowers. One little girl sold all her sampaguita and her pockets were bursting with pesos. As she played on the grass, a reflection off the ground caught her attention. She looked down and found a brand new, crisp $100 bill nestled in the grass. It should be noted that Ben Franklin, whose face appears on the $100 bill was, in his day, one of the moon's biggest fans.

Moon or no moon, balut vendors always sell plenty of their erotically charged eggs at night. On this night, though, they could not sell them fast enough. The moon had many couples feeling frisky and, combined with the magical balut, well, believe me when I tell you, many of those couples lying on the grass at Rizal Park were doing more than conversing.

The moon, of course, affected all living beings, not just the humans. At a cock fight in Tondo, a man stood outside the cockpit arena stroking his, err, ahh, cock, when he noticed his bird acting strange. The man could feel the cock was, for some reason, all juiced up. The cock was antsy and crowed like Pavarotti. He pumped his head furiously back and forth and he high-stepped across the ground. The owner, himself fond of the moon, knew an omen when he saw one. Even though his cock was a serious underdog, when fight time came, he bet heavily on him. Thanks to the moon, it was a smart bet. The cock stomped on his opponent in 20 seconds, nearly slicing his head off.

Naturally, every mosquito in town came out that night. They held a full moon party, much to the chagrin of the humans. The mosquitoes flew and bit and drank blood until they all passed out drunk. It's times like these, the humans agreed, that mosquitoes in Manila tend to overdo it a bit.

Nobody could blame the mosquitoes, though. It was not their fault. They were only reacting to a force greater than themselves. All over Manila, in every nook and in every cranny, in every hovel and in every mansion, in every field and in every garden and wherever life existed, the moon worked its enchantment in mysterious ways. Pulling and tugging at the subconscious. Making the blood boil. Waking everyone to the secrets of the night. Making magic happen.

It was not something that people really talked about. The moon is much too subtle for that. For a long time, however, people will not be able to forget the nights of the full moon over Manila.

WHEN MOM CAME TO CHECK

The term "Oi veyes mere!" is a Yiddish phrase regularly used by the world's Jewish people when they want to express complete and total exasperation over something or someone. Roughly translated, "Oi veyes mere," means the same as when a Filipino says *"Ay na ko!"* or *"Sus Maryosep!"* or when a Christian American says "Oh shit!"

On normal days, "Oi veyes mere," is not a phrase regularly heard being used at Manila's Ninoy Aquino International airport. But Tuesday, June 3rd, 1997 could hardly be considered a normal day. That was the day after Typhoon Bining left the airport without power. That was also the day when Elaine Lerner showed up.

Elaine Lerner is my mother and I had accompanied her to the airport that morning in order to try to get her on her scheduled flight out of the country. Also accompanying us were thousands upon thousands of other unfortunate, hot, annoyed, frustrated and completely baffled travelers.

"Oi veyes mere," my mother said standing amidst the not so happy throng stuck outside the departure gates. "Oi veyes mere," I said echoing her sentiments. "Ay na ko!" the Filipinos were saying. "Oh shit," the American gentiles were saying.

The airport closed, the building without power and black, the traffic backed up for miles, the heat beating down, nobody with any information to give anyone and chaos of the first degree. From us Jewish Americans, to the Filipinos, to the American gentiles, to the French, the Germans, the Aussies, the Dutch and everyone else in between, the world has probably never seen so much utter exasperation expressed in so many different languages in one place at one time ever before.

Perhaps my "Oi veyes meres" were the most vocal, however. I'm fairly used to the chaos that can arise in this country but even this was a new one. The international airport without power? The airport always has power, right? But even that I could have written off as another wild Philippine experience if not for the fact that my mother had only five days before come to the Philippines on her very first visit to the country. Why, I kept asking some unknown force, did she have to come here at the exact time when one of the worst typhoons of the decade hits the country? Why does my mother, who had come here merely to see if her baby son was Ok and that he lived in a decent place, have to endure something like this? Traffic, pollution, overcrowding, mediocre service. These we could easily explain away with a shrug and a laugh. But an entire country falling apart with my mother here? Oi veyes mere!! and then some!

Well, she did say she was coming to the Philippines to see me, not the country. That's exactly what she told me on the telephone when she called to inform me the previous April.

"Anyway," she said, "I'm not coming to see the country, I'm coming to see you." Just like that. And frankly, I wasn't surprised by the comment.

My mother has been in the travel business for the last 30 years. She and my father own a successful travel agency with seven offices in and around Allentown, Pennsylvania. In those three decades, she has done a lot of traveling and been to hundreds of cities around the world. But I don't think she has ever given a thought to vacationing in the Philippines.

Why? Well, over the years she has developed certain standards. Her hard work in the travel business has afforded her the luxury of having the finer things in life; a beautiful home, four boys through college, nice cars, fancy art on the walls and plenty of first class travel. My mother has gone to the finest places, stayed at the finest resorts, cruised on the finest ships, eaten at the finest restaurants. If it was in and trendy, my mother has been there and in style.

Believe me when I tell you that the Philippines is not exactly on the must-see list of well off, American east coast Jewish ladies who are used to having it all and having the best. The only one in my family other than myself who had stepped foot in the Philippines was my grandmother, my Mom's mother. Several years ago Ethel docked in Manila for a day while on an Orient cruise. She had these uplifting words to say about the place upon her return to the States. "Elaine, Manila is the armpit of the world!"

I was present when she said it and I did not offer even a hint of protest. Who was I to argue with my grandmother? When it comes to perfection and lavishness and classy places to go, it's no secret that you could easily think of ten places right off the bat that would come well before Manila as a destination. Very few people I know can understand why I want to live in the Philippines. Especially after having lived in Hawaii for eight years. Nobody ever says "Wow, the Philippines—that's great!" They always look at me with a big question mark on their face. They probably marvel at some perceived "sense of danger" for living in such a strange place.

I no doubt inherited my mother's taste in travel but

I suppose I rebelled against that lifestyle. Perhaps rebelled is too harsh a term. More like it never appealed
to me. Sure going five star and upscale was nice, and
still is when it comes my way. But I never found it that
interesting.

You can get five star in the Philippines, but it often
comes with everything else. There is always something
going wrong, something not quite right. Of course, those
foreigners who enjoy the Philippines generally like it
for exactly those reasons. We don't like things perfect.
Life is so much more interesting on a daily basis when
it's not predictable. To enjoy the Philippines as a foreigner, one has to have an offbeat appreciation for the
imperfections in life. You have to enjoy the fact that
you can be witness to things you did not think happened anywhere these days, even in the most primitive
of countries. Yes, the airport always has power. Or
should. When the power's out there, you know things
as a whole must be messed up and out of whack.

But just when you get totally frustrated with the
system and the chaos, you see how life simply goes on,
you see how Filipinos smile through the craziness and
continue to enjoy themselves somehow, someway and
pass it off as if it's just another day down the block. It's
all utterly brilliant. A mystery that will never make
sense. Real life in all its flawed glory. The Philippines
seduces outsiders with its veneer of western life, its
suburbs, its malls, its English speaking populace, the
way the people dress. You can get caught off guard.
Which is good because it keeps you on your toes.

Again, this is all well and good for me. I get a kick
out of it. I'm a little bit off kilter. But I did not think
my mother should have to experience this. When Mom
comes you hope and pray for a perfect time, no problems, no hassles, nothing dangerous, everything just
right. You want to make a good impression. You want

her to feel good that her son is safe and sound.

Everything started out just perfectly. In fact even before she arrived things were looking up. Mom coming from half way around the world is as good a reason as any to spruce up the house. We gave the place a nice paint job, waxed the floor, planted a few flowers along the side of the house and threw away a lot of the old junk. We even found somebody to finally fix the toilet. Hardly anyone's toilet in Manila works as it should, and now ours did. Can you imagine? A properly flushing toilet! It's amazing how a few small touches can really lift your spirits.

She was due to arrive at night which was perfect because we wouldn't have to deal with any traffic on the way to the hotel. Several days before her arrival, I went to the airport public affairs office, where they were nice enough to arrange for a personal chaperone to escort my mother through the airport. All the hassles of life in Manila be damned, I thought. We're going to wow Mom with some good old fashioned Filipino hospitality.

And it seemed to work. The escort met her as she got off the plane after traveling for nearly 24 hours from the States. When we greeted her in the lobby her first comment was, "I'm surprised, it's such a nice airport." All I can say is congratulations to the folks at the airport. My Mom's been around to a few of them and that was a helluva compliment.

Her first few days were a whirlwind of local hospitality mixed in with a healthy dose of the nagging realities of life in Manila. She loved the rooms at the Westin Philippine Plaza and thought they were very luxurious. They booked us on the 11th floor, the Premiere floor, and with the travel agent's discount, everything was just right.

One of my brother's business partners in the States is a Filipino and my Mom called up his parents to say hello. They proceeded to invite us to an exquisite dinner at the Century Chinese restaurant near the Westin.

Another day, we stopped off at my friends, the Elordes, in Parañaque, and were again treated to a big spread. Nearly the entire Elorde clan turned out to greet my Mom and this really made her feel good. "What nice people," I heard her say later.

We thought some World War II history would be nice so we looked into booking a tour to Corregidor. But when we went to the office at the Manila Bay pier, we were told that there were no half day trips because the fast boat was under repair. You had to go on the full day trip which meant a three hour boat ride in both directions and a whole day before you get back. Mom quickly nixed that one.

Like most foreigners she couldn't believe the traffic. After one day she kept repeating "looks like you could spend all day in the traffic."

Once, while we sat prisoner in another traffic snarl, something caught my Mom's attention on the sidewalk outside.

"What's with all these girls walking arm in arm like that," she said, pointing to two young women walking down the street. "Are they lesbians?" After I stopped laughing I explained that, no, they probably weren't lesbians.

"That's that old fashioned girlish thing," I said. "You know, like girls in the States used to do back in the old days."

We took Mom shopping at the SM Harrison mall which didn't impress her too much. "Stuff on the racks looks like the fashion from 20 years ago," she said. "This place must be the K-Mart here."

Unfortunately, I was not able to shield my Mom from an encounter with that famous Filipino phrase, "Sorry, out of stock." This happened on her first afternoon in

Manila while we had been cruising around in Makati.
She liked Makati, I think. She mentioned something
about how impressed she was with all the building
going on. And she seemed to like Rustans department
store, which I knew was her kind of place.

"Must be some money around here," she said while
fingering a $1,000 Nina Ricci leather bag, "This is no
cheaper than New York." This made me feel good,
because at least I knew that she now knew that not
everybody here lived in grass huts in the jungle.

After we left Rustan's my Mom insisted on buying me
a new pair of shoes. We happened upon three different
very upscale shops and, at each stop, were greeted by
the phrase, "Sorry sir, out of stock." All because we had
the nerve to ask for a size ten and a half.

"What, is size ten such a big deal here?" my Mom
asked. "Why is every place out of stock?"

"No big deal," I said. "It's the custom around here."

The next day we rented a van with a driver and took
a trip to Tagaytay. There we met my sister-in-law who
happens to be a member of the Tagaytay Highlands
Country Club. Now this was more like my mother's
style. Tagaytay Highlands is a lavish, opulent country
club that looks like it was built by Walt Disney. It has
a majestic golf course impossibly built on the side of a
mountain, a sports club with bowling, squash, lap pool,
grass tennis courts, pony rides, massage therapists,
six restaurants on site, giant and beautiful gardens, a
plant nursery that could rival any in the world, a gon-
dola that ferries you up and down the mountain and
a mountain top bar that can only be reached by cable
car. And indeed my mother went wild.

"I've been to a lot of nice places," she said with an in-
credulous look on her face, "but I've never seen a place
like this. It's lavish. Somebody has some money around
here. You'd never know it driving up here."

We spent the afternoon at Tagaytay Highlands and were having a snack on the veranda when the nasty weather hit. We decided to leave and my sister-in-law said she knew a short cut to the South Superhighway that would save us an hour getting back to Manila and that we should follow her. The road was a typical Philippine province road that goes from being paved to unpaved about ten different times. There were no lights and the van bobbed up and down in the pot holes as we moved slowly along.

"How can we come from such a nice place and the road looks like this?" my Mom asked.

"Welcome to the Philippines," was the response from my wife. Then my sister-in-law's van got stuck going over the edge where the pavement ended. In the darkness and rain I got out with the driver to help her get her van out of the rut. Several other drivers got out to help. I noticed my mother was laughing. At least she was rolling with the punches.

Sunday we rented a taxi and took a trip up to the former Clark Air Base in Angeles City for the day. On the way there the deluge started.

"Maybe we should turn back," Mom said sounding worried.

"Don't worry," I assured her, "this kind of rain is common here." Ahh, little did I know. I guess Mom does know best.

At Clark she despised the duty free shops, was impressed by the golf course and hotel and again mentioned that "somebody around here has deep pockets." After an awful lunch at the Holiday Inn, we decided to head back to Manila. As we hit Quezon City, though, we ran into floods and traffic.

"My god, what kind of life is this?" Mom cried. "What is it that you like about this place?" After navigating through several newly formed lakes on the streets of

Manila and finally reaching the Westin, my mother quipped, "I tell you what, tomorrow I don't want to even get in a car. Let's just stay around the hotel."

That's exactly what we did. For we had no choice. Monday came, the rain poured down in buckets and the wind howled. Typhoon Bining was upon us.

"This is unbelievable," Mom said as she stared out the window of her room at the waves crashing against the sea wall and the coconut trees bent to the ground. "I may not be able to get out of here tomorrow." Uh oh, this was getting serious. I told Au to take her shopping. That way she could relax and buy some *pasalubong* (gifts) for the folks back home.

My Mom and Au left for Harrison Plaza in the morning while I stayed behind to do some work. They couldn't find a cab and were forced to take a jeepney in the middle of a typhoon. At Harrison Plaza my mother saw water dripping from the ceiling and immediately wanted to leave because she thought the building might collapse.

Later back at the hotel, she wanted to get information about the weather, especially since she was leaving the next day. We turned on the television and found one local newscast. The lady came on and gave graphic details of the thirteen people who died so far. She told all the bloody details of how, where and when they died. But she gave no weather report.

We tried calling Northwest Airlines but nobody answered the phone. After some time she got through but the agent said there was no number to call after hours regarding cancellations. We turned on the flight information channel to see if the airport was still open but the channel merely listed the arriving and departing flights.

"What is it you like about this place?" Mom kept asking.

The weather slowed that night and we left for the

airport the next morning at 4:45 am. Mom's flight was scheduled to leave at 7:30 am. We sailed along until we reached the entrance to the airport where, suddenly, everything came to a standstill. Dawn was breaking and I noticed the airport was completely dark.

"It doesn't even look open," I said. We were able to turn into the airport but the traffic came to a halt. "Let's walk," I said. We paid the taxi driver and I grabbed my Mom's suitcase from the trunk. We walked up the ramp to the departure area where we were confronted with one of the strangest scenes I've ever witnessed; thousands upon thousands of people waiting outside a darkened airport. I had never before seen an international airport with no electricity. Neither did my mother.

"This is a disgrace," she said shaking her head. "Oi veyes mere."

Black, dark, like an empty shell of someone's monument to grandeur. It was weird. I drive by the airport a lot and always assume that it is the one place that, no matter what happens, will always have power. They've always got something at the airport, a secret airport electricity button, or their own indestructible power station with five back-ups, or some super battery that big airports the world over have buried under the terminal or runway. That's why I like living close to the airport, I always told myself. I figure I have a quick out if something horrific like an earthquake levels Manila and all but cuts the place off from the rest of the world.

But assumptions die hard in Manila and I should have reminded myself that the phrase, "You would think…" doesn't readily apply. It was as if the country didn't exist for a few moments. Indeed one stranded, Camel-smoking Dutch toy merchant told us how he had come to the airport the day before on Monday, checked in, cleared immigration and was sitting in the departure lounge waiting for his flight to Hong Kong when the power went out. His flight was then cancelled and he went to leave the airport.

"On the way out," he said chuckling between drags, "we had to go back through the immigration section so we could get back into the country. But when we got there, nobody was manning the counters. The immigration people had all gone home. So I just left the airport and went back to Makati. Technically I'm in the country illegally."

Also trying unsuccessfully to get to Hong Kong for over a day was the large, perspiring Indian businessman who stood with his sport coat draped over his shoulder and a resigned grin on his face. He claimed he worked for a large multinational that consulted for power companies and said he was involved in the deal that sold the now-not-working equipment to the Philippine government.

"How could something like this happen?" I asked him. "I thought the airport was the one place that always had power."

He laughed. "You're right but obviously they didn't do something right when they installed the equipment. Maybe the government engineer underestimated something. Who knows? But they did something wrong I can tell you that. I've been to places like Bangladesh, India and Pakistan, and I've never seen anything like this."

We tried to get solid information but all we could get was rumor. We heard the airport was opening at 7:30, 10 o'clock, at three in the afternoon. We found two pay phones and tried to call Northwest Airlines. But the one phone didn't work and the other one only offered free calls to the operator. At this point my mother could just laugh.

"What is it that you like about this place?" she asked.

I laughed as well. "I guess you have to have an appreciation for life's imperfections," I said, finally figuring out how to answer her.

"Well, I'm going to miss my connections," she said, "but I'm not worried about that. I just want to get out of this place." Finally after five hot and stuffy hours standing outside the terminal, someone came out and called all passengers on Northwest Airlines' flight to Osaka. In the ensuing crush to the terminal entrance, my Mom made it through but I got left behind with her bag. Some kind soul in the fray grabbed the bag, put it on his head and handed it to my Mom. I was then able to squeeze through and give my Mom a big hug and kiss.

"Thanks for coming Mom," I said. We looked at each other and both laughed again.

"My pleasure," she said. "Whew, what a place." With that she turned and headed into the now lighted but still boiling terminal. I didn't, and still don't, expect to see her come out from that same terminal any time soon.

"I've had my heart broken by so many foreigners. Two Aussies, one German. They all promise to marry me and take me to their country. But they make bola bola. You know what is bola bola?"

"Yeh, they bullshitted you," I say laughing. "It's part of the game don't you think?"

5

CONVERSATION WITH A BAR GIRL

The sound of pumping dance music fills the large, smoky, ultra modern room, while neon lights flash on and off and spin around. Up on the stage, which is directly behind the bar, over thirty girls, all dressed in skimpy black and white string bikinis and black, knee-high, high heeled boots, move and gyrate to the music.

Nearly every seat at the bar is taken and most of the tables and booths are filled as well. Most of the customers look to be foreigners—white guys, several black guys, a handful of Japanese—but there also appears to be a few Filipinos here. Some of the men sip drinks and eye the dancers. The girls return friendly smiles. Other men sit and talk with some of the bikini clad girls. In one booth a girl sits on an older guy's lap.

Lourdes leans against the stand up counter, stirring her drink with a straw. The neon and black lights make her skin appear a deep dark brown while the white in her bikini, as well as her teeth and eyes, look electrified. Her thick mane of long, shiny black hair cascades down the side of her pretty face and over her bare shoulder, barely touching the counter top. She says she's 23 years old, from the Bicol region, and has worked in bars like this since she was 19. She lights up a cigarette and takes a puff.

"I like the bar I guess," she says while blowing smoke. "It's Ok. I like meeting all the different people. I make friends with all the girls. But I'm only doing it so I can put myself through school. I want to be a nurse. I'm working here four nights a week.

"I've had my heart broken by so many foreigners. Two Aussies, one German. They all promise to marry me and take me to their country. But they make *bola bola*. You know what is bola bola?"

"Yeh, they bullshitted you," I say laughing. "It's part of the game don't you think?"

"I suppose," she says as she takes a drag. "I don't know. One Australian guy, he's a big businessman. Has plenty of money. He's always flying all over the world. When he comes to Manila he always come see me. But he don't like me working in the bar so he give me money to go to school. I don't ask from him, but he give me money so I can help my parents. Our house in Tabaco was damaged very badly in the typhoon. And I'm helping with my brothers and sisters. I'm thinking he is a very nice man. He promised to marry me and take care of me and my family. Then one day he tells me he can't see me anymore because he has a wife and children in Australia. I was so upset I cried for three days."

"How about the other guys?" I ask.

"The German was a factory worker," she says. "From Munich. He was a young guy. He came here, it was his first time in the Philippines. He took me out of the bar. We went to Boracay. Then he took me to Puerto Galera. He told me he loved me and wanted to marry me. He sent money two times from Germany and wrote in his letter that I should wait for him, that he will come back and marry me and take me back to Germany. But then I never hear from him anymore. He just stopped writing. I tried to call him collect but I don't speak German. I think it was a wrong number. I think foreigners are crazy people."

"Maybe you're driving them crazy," I say.

"Me? No, I'm a very loving person. I just don't understand these men. The other Aussie came to visit me several times. He would take me traveling. He also promised to marry me. While I was with him, I got pregnant. Then he disappeared. I never saw him again."

"What happened to the baby?"

"I drank some medicine and got rid of it."

"Do you have a boyfriend now?"

"Well not really. One guy was a black guy, he work at the US Embassy. But I don't like blacks. He wants to make boom-boom six times in one night. He's too strong. I cannot take it. Anyway, I have no feeling for blacks. I like white guys. I don't know, I think he's crazy. Americans are nice but they like sex too much. They always want sex."

"How about you?" I ask.

"Well I like sex," she says with a giggle. "Yes, I'm horny. Sometimes. But not like that. I like white guys. I mean if I have a feeling for the guy, then I'm wild in bed. I have no problem with it. I used to sleep in the same room with my parents. I'm the oldest child of six kids. We all sleep in the same room. And sometimes I would see my parents doin' it. They never said it was bad or anything. Even though the priest and nuns used to say it was wrong. But my mom and dad, they sometimes did it. So I guess it was no big deal. But he's too horny. I think Americans are crazy."

"Probably a lot of them, sure."

"I used to have another boyfriend who would come and see me, he was from the Embassy too."

"Where did you meet him?"

"In the bar. Then after I meet him, I stop working in the bar. We lived together in Malate (a neighborhood near Ermita in Manila) for a year and a half. He calls me sometimes. And sometimes he comes in here to see me. But he don't like me working in the bar."

"Well why are you working here, did he do something?"

"I find out he has another girlfriend," she says. "So I left him."

"When was this?"

"Just two weeks ago."

"Did you like him?"

"Yes I used to like him very much. He promised he would marry me and take me to America. I thought his heart was with me. But then I find out he has another girl friend. I ask him about it and he first say no, but then he say he did. He knows that I know. So he say that's just the way he is. So I moved out."

"So you don't like it if your boyfriend wants to go short-time with another girl?"

"Short-time? It's Ok with me. As long as he tells me. He want to pay a bar fine, that's Ok. So long as he tells me. But if he don't tell me and I find out, that's no good. So long as his heart is with me."

"What was his job at the Embassy?"

"He stamps the passports so Filipinos can go to the States. I used to ask him when we would marry and go to America. But he keep saying "later, later." He say now too many Filipinos want to go to America. He always tell me about America and how I would really like it there. He say it's the promise land. So I tell him we just go for a visit. He stamps the passport, right? So I told him I will get a passport and he can stamp it. But he says he can't do that. Then he always tell me he love me so much. Then I find out he has another girlfriend. So I left him." She shakes her head and looks in to her drink. "I don't understand foreigners. They come here and make too much butterfly."

"Sounds like you were angry," I say.

"I'm *naiinis*," she says raising her voice. "You know what is naiinis? I'm very pissed off. While I'm packing my things I yell at him. So I say 'Why you come here in my country and make boom-boom with me, but you can't take me to the States?' I tell him he's probably the guy who don't allow my auntie to visit her dying mother in America. I tell him that my auntie tell me that the man behind the window at the Embassy don't even look at her papers. He just said no. My auntie tell me that the US Embassy steals P500 from so many Filipinos and don't even give them a chance. Now he comes in here and tells me he's sorry and that he loves me again. I told him, 'Fuck your country! I don't want to stay in your country!' He's always saying that America is the promise land. Yeh, everybody's full of promises!"

ON AN ORDINARY FRIDAY NIGHT

It was a sultry, moon washed Friday night as I stood outside the Seven-Eleven along Sucat Rd. in Parañaque eating a penoy. I had just bought the warm egg from the friendly butch-lady balut vendor who nightly sits right outside the store and sells her magical eggs, along with single cigarettes, which she buys by the pack from inside the Seven-Eleven.

I downed my penoy, paid the butch-lady and walked to the curb, where I tried to flag a jeepney. My watch read just past 11:30 but, still, the night pulsed with action. Many vehicles jockeyed for position on the road, and several people stood on the curb trying to get rides. Three jeeps passed me by and picked up other passengers. Another noticed me standing there and stopped, but his jeep looked full and I waved him on. Just then, another pulled up and stopped right in front of me. This jeepney was only three-quarters full, so I quickly climbed in the back and took a seat.

The jeepney pulled out into traffic and headed down Sucat Rd. towards the South Expressway. It was a typically average jeepney, semi-rundown but clean. The faded red vinyl seats were mostly nice but showed signs of wear with a few tatters and tears. The floor was worn and rough, while the metal ceiling shined. On the front hood a metal horse stood proudly perched. From the rear view mirror hung rosary beads, a small statue of Jesus on the cross and a green, tree-shaped, cardboard air freshener.

Outside the darkened, dirty, closed down buildings streamed past and reminded me how so very ugly and desperate Manila can look, especially at night. I checked out the people joining me inside the jeepney. To my right sat a thin lady in her late 30's and her five or six year old daughter who lay asleep on mom's lap. The mother held a colorful woven shopping bag which rested on the floor and was filled halfway with various things inside plastic bags. On my left sat two middle aged men in shorts, T-shirts and rubber slippers. They both held unlighted cigarettes in their hands.

Across from me a security guard just off work sat semi-slumped and staring out into space. He wore a

white T-shirt and held his blue work shirt in his hand. He looked completely exhausted as he tried to fight off an attack of yawning. A little ways down, two girls in their 20's sat close to each other with arms linked, each with a hand resting on the other's leg. Next to them sat a woman in her 50's clutching a small black purse and a long green umbrella. In the back of the jeepney, by the entrance, was a young guy who looked to be a dance instructor. He had short, slicked-back, black hair and wore nicely pressed white pants, shiny black shoes, a white button down shirt, a thin black tie and he carried a small handbag.

Just an ordinary jeepney, I thought, plying the busy road with a bunch of ordinary people on any old Friday night in Manila. Or was it? It was several minutes before I began noticing something different, something unique about this jeepney. At first I thought it could have been that this jeepney had been mildly dressed up and it was actually nice inside. Then I noticed that the stereo was on and its sound came through the speakers loud and crystal clear. And as if to compliment the horse motif on the hood, the voice of Glen Campbell filled up the jeepney.

"Like a rhinestone cowboy," Glen sang at full volume, *"Riding out on my horse to a star spangled rodeo ..."* I smiled to myself at this slice of Americana inside a Philippine jeepney. But then I noticed that Glen was not singing by himself. I turned towards the voice and realized it was the driver and he was singing loudly, as if he were singing a duet with Glen Campbell.

Yes, it was the jeepney driver who was the key to this whole scene. From what I could see, he looked to be in his mid-40's and slightly overweight. He was wearing a sleeveless, white *sando* T-shirt and a checkered fedora hat. Interestingly, I thought, he had his lady with him. She also looked to be in her 40's. She wore a sleeveless, turquoise sun dress that showed off an ample cleavage and made her look kind of sexy.

Together they made a great couple. He sat semi-reclining, with about a quarter of his body to the right of the steering wheel in that near right angle that almost all jeepney drivers position themselves. His right shoulder leaned up against his woman, who sat in the middle of the front seat, even though the seat next to her, the one where the passenger has one foot resting on the dash outside, was empty. *"Like a rhinestone cowboy ..."* He sang loudly with Glen.

They were mere inches away from leaning their heads together and, with him singing, I thought for a moment that they looked like they could be the happiest couple on earth. This was their Friday night together. He drives, she tags along to keep him company, she takes the money from the passengers, she keeps a hand on his thigh, he sings her songs.

A few passengers had gotten off and we seemed to be close to the South Expressway, the end of the route. We had run into heavy traffic, though, and the jeepney sat absolutely still, surrounded by cars, trucks, and other jeepneys. The next thing I knew, I heard the unmistakable voice of Nat King Cole come over the stereo. The sound was so clear, Nat sounded as if he was sitting next to me on the jeepney. And the driver joined right in.

"The night is like a lovely tune," sang Nat and the driver in slow, lilting unison as the jeepney idled in the traffic, *"Beware my foolish heart. How wise the ever constant moon. Take care my foolish heart."*

As the boys crooned and the driver's woman no doubt swooned, I tried to check out the scene outside. The narrow, low windows of the jeepney only allowed glimpses but it was clearly urban madness as only Manila knows it. On the one side I was face to face with the huge dirty wheels of a tractor trailer truck, which had come right up to the window. Outside the other window, the world teemed with people. Some walked in, out and between the jeepneys, cars, and trucks. Others cruised up and down the side of the road.

"There's a line between love and fascination, that's hard to see on an evening such as this. For they both give the very same sensation, when you're lost in the magic of a kiss."

The jeepney inched slowly forward, in perfect unison with the golden, silky-smooth voice of Nat King Cole and his baritone jeepney driver partner, whose woman leaned lazily on his shoulder. I spotted a night market by the side of the road. People sold vegetables and fruits under bare bulbs strung up in a row in front of *carinderias* (canteens) advertising Coke and Sprite. A crowd was gathered around a vendor frying fish balls. Thick smoke billowed off a grill barbecuing sticks of pork. A group of five men sat at a table and played cards with a half empty bottle of rum waiting to be finished off. A pile of garbage lay around a nearby telephone pole. People moved in every direction, cutting through the dust, dirt, soot and noise that filled the air.

"Her lips are much too close to mine, beware my foolish heart. But should our eager lips combine, then let the fire start."

We were in the middle of total Third World chaos, a virtual urban hell, a definite future-gone-mad scenario, but it mattered little. For the driver had made this cozy little jeepney his own slice of heaven that made it seem worlds away from the craziness happening just outside. It was as if we were frozen in time. Like I was an extra in a "B" movie being filmed at exactly that moment.

"For this time it isn't fascination, or a dream that will fade and fall apart. It's love ... this time it's love ... my

foolish heart."

The song over, I tapped on the ceiling and yelled *"para"* (stop). Just before I jumped out the back and into the hot, dusty fray outside, I called, *"Salamat!"* It was a thank you to the driver for stopping and picking me up and for bringing me, if only for a few moments, into his magical little world within a world on that very ordinary Friday night.

RAINDROPS KEEP FALLING ON MY BRAIN

I have never been one to begrudge the odd rainy day here and there. Actually, I rather enjoy them. When it comes at the occasional expense of constant sun, the rain offers a relaxing change of mood. The rain can take you away from the hustle and bustle of daily life. The rain says, "No problem, stay in bed for a while. It's Ok to be lazy and do nothing today."

Like so many other occasions, Filipinos like the rain because it's another reason for a fiesta. And, almost as importantly, the wet weather gives Filipinos a chance to wear winter clothing. Even though in reality things are nearly as balmy and warm as any other day in the tropics, the wet weather offers Filipinos an excuse to break out their heaviest woolens, long underwear, sweaters, ski parkas and mittens and imagine for a moment what it might be like to live in New York in January. They sit in cafés and carinderias bundled up in sweatshirts, L. L. Bean type jackets, and knit hats and eat hot soup and drink coffee. Perhaps while sitting there, they look at the coconut trees and try to imagine large icicles hanging from the branches.

I have always wondered if Filipinos actually feel bone chillingly cold during the prolonged stretches of rainy weather, or if they just like making a fashion statement. I suspect the latter. Any chance for Filipinos to make a fashion statement is a chance that will, more than likely, not be missed. Although I will grant the possibility they could really be feeling cold. The rain has the very powerful ability to play with your mind like that.

As for me, I think I now understand why they call these weather systems tropical depressions. Because they can easily make you depressed. This would make sense because, after all, we are living beings—well, some of us anyway—and if the atmospheric pressure were low, we would also feel low.

But it's not just one storm. Again one storm is always kind of nice. It's really the constant driving rain, everyday, all day and with no end in sight. Man, can it ever rain in the Philippines! The rain here does not just simply fall. It pours down in sheets, fast and heavy. Its intensity is equaled in strength only by its duration, which when combined, makes for an awesome and indescribable force of nature.

I recall one particular two week stretch of non-stop hard driving rain that had me in awe. And in a state of misery, as well. Day after day after day after wet, dark and dreary day left me a defeated man. The consistent intensity of the rain made me want to cry. After a while, the water that fell from the sky seemed to seep inside my brain. This, I believe, is what scientists call "water on the brain."

Familiar people and known places looked different. I started to feel desperate, somehow closed in. I started to feel the way a bear must feel with winter fast approaching and all he can think of is hibernating for a few months until it all passes.

The first thing I tried to do to combat this feeling was to go out and occupy my mind by running a few errands. This turned out to be a big mistake. I did not last more than an hour. The rain came down in buckets. The streets of Manila were completely flooded and several times the car fell into nasty potholes that could not be

seen because they were filled with water. And having
to look at this pitifully ugly city rendered even uglier
by the dreary weather, made me even more down. One
might think that the rain would cleanse the city and
perhaps make it clean for a day or two. But the rains
and the floods actually carry all the garbage into full
view. It all had me feeling trapped and I realized that
it was very possible that any trip too far away from
home could easily turn into a quagmire of traffic and
gridlock. In Manila the rains could literally keep you
from getting back home for days. I quickly turned back
and headed for home.

Stuck at home and unwilling to venture very far,
I had to find ways to amuse myself. I had to try and
break the severe rainy day blahs. I tried reading a book
but felt so depressed, I could not concentrate. I read a
few newspapers and, naturally, things became worse.
This was around the time the Olympics were happening and I thought that might clear my foul mood. But
the antenna cord on my television broke and I couldn't
receive any channels.

I then went to the video shop down the block to pick
up a couple of those pirated VHS movies. There I got
suckered by the erotic language on the box and ended
up renting something called 'Boxing Helena,' which
turned out to be a dark and depressing tale of some
sexually repressed, rich surgeon who becomes obsessed
over some good-looking vamp down the block. In the
movie, the doctor makes these childish and wimpish
advances which the woman always rudely spurns. Then
the woman ridiculously ends up getting hit by a car
while leaving the doctor's dreary mansion. The doctor,
hopelessly whipped, sees his big opportunity and takes
his injured infatuation into the house and operates. To
save her life, he has to amputate both her legs, and one
arm. Awful for her, but certainly not for him. Because

she cannot go anywhere, he now gets to take care of her for the rest of his life! How pleasant!

Was somebody trying to tell me something? Now I felt madness approaching. I felt like I was up against the wall. And all the while the rain did not let up.

I found some solace in finding fun ways to massacre all the vermin who invaded the house because of the heavy rains. With the rains the ants, cockroaches, and mice came in droves. I'm not sure if this is because all their usual haunts had been flooded out, or because all their regular food sources, like rat supermarkets and cockroach convenience stores, had been washed away.

Either way, they quickly figured out where not to take refuge the next time the rains leave their lair flooded. The cockroaches who came to visit me learned to let their fingers do the walking as I pulled out a time-tested American technique; the Yellow Pages. That's always been a handy book to have around the house, in more ways than one. Next time you want to have fun ridding your house of cockroaches, just grab the Yellow Pages, hold it with both hands high over your head and then slam it down on top of that vile bug with all the force you can muster. I guarantee that the cockroach will instantly be rendered into cockroach mulch. Just make sure you have a tissue handy to clean the bottom of the book. Mashed cockroaches leave quite a mess.

The way the ants like to congregate around one spot, the Yellow Pages would have been a perfect tool to slaughter them all at once. But I didn't want to abuse the poor book. After all, I still have to use it sometimes for its intended purpose. So instead I would leave a small morsel of fish on the kitchen counter and wait for about 30 minutes for the ant regiment to show up. Then out would come a boiling hot, soaking wet sponge. As the ants fell en masse I imagined how the Six O'clock

Ant News would have a breaking story about a major catastrophe in the ant community today.

As far as the fate of the mice—or baby rats if you will—well, they too did not stand a chance. To rid the house of mice, I placed some nice sticky fly paper right in the middle of their favorite thoroughfares. This is an incredibly effective method as it often only takes several minutes for the mice to run across the paper and get stuck. And the sounds of them squealing in horror as they writhe and wiggle on the paper is surely enough to scare the living hell out of all the other rats in and around the house and let them know that it would be best if they got the hell out now and immediately told all their relatives never to visit again.

I imagine Filipinos reading this are having a good laugh at my expense and this I can understand. Unlike the States where, when people see ants crawling around the kitchen counter they go into spasmodic convulsions, Filipinos never seem to make a big deal about having to share their home with bugs, mice, and rats. And after having lived in the Philippines for some time, I, too, have softened my stand on their right to exist. But with the rains falling endlessly, leaving not only my body but my mind trapped, I obviously was being driven close to the edge.

And this reign of terror did nothing to cure my foul mood, which festered in the wet air. I began to feel like I was committing mass murder. I then turned my attention to the dog, Shiggy, a horny pure white spitz, who, at the same time the rains were falling, gave birth to four ugly black and white mutts.

Birth should be a happy event, but I was actually ticked at Shiggy for schtuping any two-timing mutt that comes along and then bringing more mangy mouths into the world to feed.

Several hours after giving birth, one of Shiggy's puppies died. When Shiggy realized what had happened, she proceeded to eat the dead baby. Not only did this highly disgust me, it perplexed me and worsened my frame of mind. I did not know that dogs ate their dead young. You can imagine what this would do to you even if you were of sane mind. Imagine how I must have felt having been completely depressed and the rain continuing to pour incessantly.

Then on Friday, after several extended torrential downpours, the house got flooded. Funny, but this seemed to turn things around for me. I suddenly realized that before the flood, I was at the mercy of Mother Nature and she had me feeling helpless and sorry for myself. But with the flood, I fought back. And I suddenly had a real place to vent my angst. As we swept water out of the living room and cleaned up the resulting mess, we cursed the Gatchalian real estate people for building subdivisions without proper drainage. Hopefully they are reading this and feel ashamed of themselves.

After several hours we managed to get things relatively cleaned and back in place. The skies were still ominous, but I was feeling strangely light. That night I went out on the town and partied until dawn. I had finally broken the rainy day blues. It's good to think that perhaps one of those rain clouds had a silver lining.

FROM MY CORNER WINDOW

Our new apartment in Parañaque is a typical two-bedroom concrete abode with a medium-sized living area/kitchen downstairs and two bedrooms upstairs. Certainly nothing special except for one thing: the apartment is the corner unit overlooking the quiet dead-end road of the small village.

I consider myself a simple man. Don't require too many material things to be comfortable. One thing I love, though, is that perch above the action. Of course, one of the upstairs rooms is the bedroom. The other is where I throw all my crap. That room is also where I work, or rather, stare out of the windows, daydream and wait until the deadline approaches before I get down to work.

It's also where I check out the scene. The corner unit offers me windows on two sides and it also affords me a direct, birds eye view of this small village. There's a fair amount of action here, although, perhaps "action" is the wrong word. It's more like typical daily life in a quiet city village in Manila.

We literally live "at the end of the road." That last phrase is in quotes because "end of the road" is generally a nice way of saying you're down and out, you're on the streets, wherever you lay your hat is your home. Well, we have a paid roof over our heads. It's just that it literally sits at the end of the road, three rights and three lefts down a poorly marked, narrow lane and well away from the busy highway. There is no thru-road through our village.

From my corner window I can see the tops of coconut trees and water tanks in this village and over in the next village. On certain days I can look down the street and see the old men sitting on worn wooden benches, their T-shirts rolled up around their bulbous bellies, quietly sipping their Gilbey's Gin and lime juice. As the day wears on, they become louder, they laugh a lot and they start to do that drunken lean.

From my corner window, I can see grimy kids scurrying around on the potholed pavement. Sometimes I see them come up to the outside of our gate, ring our doorbell and run away laughing. The first time I saw them do this I got a little irritated, until I realized that one of my favorite activities as a kid was ringing people's doorbells and running away in hysterics.

On some afternoons, I can see young guys kicking back under a run-down waiting shed playing cards. At night, several teenagers gather regularly up the block and sit on benches under the street lamp and play guitar and sing songs. Their repertoire consists of perhaps five songs—two Air Supply songs, two Michael Learns to Rock songs and one Tagalog love song. They do not sing too bad, if only they would learn a few more tunes.

From my corner window I can watch the comings and goings of the residents here. A major daily activity is walking to a sari-sari store to buy Coke and cigarettes. It's amazing how sari-sari stores are hidden in every corner of the village. Although, as a newcomer here, it's been difficult to tell if you're at a sari-sari store or the merchandise you see on the shelf outside somebody's front door is simply for their personal use. My first week here I saw some canned goods and bags of chips sitting on a table just inside the gate of somebody's house. I knocked and a lady came out. When she saw my empty bottle of Coke, she shook her head and pointed to the store three houses away.

From my corner window I can watch the bicycle pedicabs roll in and out—thankfully tricycles are not allowed here—and marvel at just how it is they make a living. I also marvel at how the people who ride these pedicabs are too lazy to make the 10-minute walk from the main road.

At night, the pedicab drivers often park their bikes outside my window in the dusty, dirty empty lot next to the apartment. There they listen to the radio and sleep inside their pedicabs in impossible positions. That lot is also where the village dogs, as well as dogs from all over Parañaque it seems, hang out. The dogs around here are certifiably mad. Rarely can they be seen during the day. At night, though, when the village begins to quiet down, the dogs come out in force, constantly barking, fighting and bickering for the stupidest of reasons.

When we first moved in here a few months back, the nonstop noise of the dogs nearly made me pack up and leave within a week. The first night here, I opened up all the windows in the bedroom in order to enjoy the cross ventilation that comes with having the coveted corner unit. But we were perched directly over the street, and the only thing that got ventilated through was the racket of the dogs. It felt like I had moved into a pet shop instead of an apartment. My angry shouts from the window threatening to shoot every last one of the mangy mutts only made them more crazed. So we installed an air conditioner. Not so much to cool the room, but because I'd rather listen to the hum of the air-con than a symphony of psychotic canines.

From my corner window I can watch as the various characters wander through trying to extract a few pesos from the residents. This village is practically hidden and yet, still, they manage to find us back here. The general quiet of this village is constantly being interrupted throughout the day by people selling their wares. Not that I mind really. It's always interesting to see what people have to sell. And it's also nice to know that in this malled-out world of ours, good old-fashioned peddling is alive and well. And yes, I am a willing buyer, at times.

Whether regulars or newcomers, all hawkers let the village know of their presence by shouting into the air or, as is the case with the ice cream guys, ringing a bell. The first one early in the morning is the fish lady who rides her pedicab back in here between eight and nine o'clock. She's a friendly lady who always brings something different and doesn't mind giving a little credit if you're short on cash.

About the same time, the man selling 'taho' (sweet tofu snack) strolls by. I love to watch his routine as he's very particular about how he serves the taho. After putting down his two large silver buckets, he carefully scoops out the excess water from the warm taho and throws it on the ground. Then, after placing the taho in a plastic cup, he opens one half of the other large silver drum and scoops on some 'sago' (jelly-like beans). From the other side he scoops out a ladle of sweet brown syrup. For five pesos I consider it a steal.

Sometime a little later in the morning comes the guy selling *gulay*(vegetables.) He pushes one of those long wooden carts with the tiny wobbly wheels that looks like it will fall apart at any moment. He manages to fit a stunning array of vegetables into that cart and he has a bit of a dashing air about him. He always dresses in a brightly colored sando T-shirt tucked into checkered shorts. His most notable trait is the wicker hat that says "Baguio, Philippines," on the brim.

Between eleven o'clock and one, the shoe repair man

makes his appearance. He doesn't only attend to shoes. If you have a broken umbrella or hand bag he can handle that as well. One of the best things about this guy is the way he lets you know he's around. He has one of the best calls of any of the vendors. You can hear him coming from way down the street as he howls into the air. "Zapatos!! (shoes), Zapatos!!" He says it with this semi-whiny tone while lingering on the first syllable, "Zaaaapatos!! Zaaaapatos!!" My day is not complete without hearing the *zapatos* man pass by.

Between one to four o'clock come several ice cream men, either pushing a cart or pedaling a pedicab. With ice cream it's clear you've got to have good timing. There's only so much of it a small village can eat. One Sunday, I sat upstairs and saw the guy with the push cart selling "Koolcreme" ice cream come through. He practically sold out his entire inventory. About a half an hour after he left, another ice cream guy came here on his pedicab and got completely shut out.

At around three o'clock, of course, it's time for *merienda* (afternoon snack). Everyday a man peddles through shouting "*puto at kutsinta*!!" (rice cakes). Several days a week another man walks by carrying a native tray of barbecued bananas on sticks. "Banana-que! Banana-que!"

By night fall, of course, it's time for the ever-present balut vendor. We have two balut vendors who pass through. Several times a night I can hear their long drawn-out cries fill the sultry night air of the village as they pedal their small BMX bicycles, weighed down with their baskets of warm, magical eggs, up and down the block.

In between the regulars, come the others, some new-comers, some you see only once in a while. Occasionally a lady strolls through selling *tinapa* (small smoked fish). The smelly fish are sealed in plastic and she sells the packages right out of her large hand bag.

The other people always have something different to sell. From my corner window upstairs I can see them all pass by. As I've been typing this piece some loud mouth came through carrying gaudy mirrors and paintings of the Last Supper. Once a week we're sure to get a man who hands over a piece of paper explaining that he is collecting donations for the blind, the deaf, the homeless or some other charity. The other day one old man, whom I saw two weeks before hawking pots and pans, came to our door selling every size plastic bucket imaginable. Funny, but our water pump had just gone on the blink and we needed a bucket and he made a sale.

A few days back I was sitting upstairs typing, well, mostly staring out of the window, when an army of people came through peddling laundry detergent. They pulled up in a van with a voice blaring out of the loud speaker on the roof. At first I thought it was a promotion by a politician trying to win the women's vote by handing out free laundry detergent. They walked up and down the street banging on everybody's gate. I only realized it was strictly a sales promotion when I discovered the deal was buy two boxes, take one free. If it was a political deal, the detergent would have been handed out at no cost, of course.

Easily the biggest activity of the day in this village is the buying, selling, delivery and carrying of water. Five minutes sitting at my desk and several jeepneys and owner-style jeeps dragging big dripping water tanks drive in, park for a few minutes and then leave. They come constantly from dawn until well into the night. No doubt the neighbors are doing a nice business. And it never fails to amaze me how Filipinos spend an inordinately large portion of their day dealing with something as basic as water.

I have also discovered that my corner perch is ideal for checking out one of life's rarely seen or experienced phenomena. It's called the "blue hour." Not many people know about the blue hour, but it surely exists. The blue hour is the time of day when it's not night and it's not day. It occurs in the deepest part of the night and the earliest part of the morning. It's that point where night just ends and morning has yet to begin. Not midnight. Closer to 4 a.m. or thereabouts.

The blue hour only lasts for a fraction of a second, but when it occurs, simultaneously on the edge of night and the edge of day, neither really, the entire world comes to a halt and there is complete and total silence. Neither roosters, nor dogs, nor any other living thing can be heard. A moment later the world explodes into a new day and the blue hour is gone.

Most people are asleep at that time or, if they are awake, are not paying attention. I once happened to be awake at that time and I found myself staring out of the second floor window looking out over the trees into the dark sky. And there it was. For one precious moment the world had come to a complete halt. The wind died, the roosters and dogs went silent, cars or planes couldn't be heard. Incredibly, Manila was dead silent. And then it was over. Morning had begun. A glimpse of some magic right from my corner window.

THE SOUNDS THAT REVEAL

L ook, and you see action; several dozen bare-chested young guys jump, pound, skip, bend, stretch and punch in a relentless training session that has sweat pouring from their bodies.

Take a whiff and you smell that sweat, from today and days long past, combined with the rank odor of urine emanating from the toilets at the back. It's a hard-core smell, but not necessarily bad considering, after all, that this is an old boxing gym.

If you try to feel this scene, you feel one thing: heat. Outside the midday sun beats down on the pavement. It has not rained in weeks and the air has a veneer of dry dust and is searing hot.

But of all the senses that get turned on in a boxing gym—this is the Elorde Boxing Gym in the basement of the Elorde Sports Center in Parañaque, Metro Manila; but it could be anywhere in the world—the one that becomes most acute is the sense of hearing. As I sit in the small wooden bleachers, surrounded by several copies of the day's tabloids and next to two guys playing cards and smoking Marlboros, I cannot help but listen to the sounds. It's the sounds that stand out in a gym, that tell the true story of what's happening; the hard slapping of leather fists pounding old heavy leather bags, the rhythmic snap and patter of jump ropes hitting the worn, wood parquet floor, the rapid fire crackling of the speed bag, the pounding of feet as boxers spar inside the two run down rings.

But it's the sounds between rounds that are the most graphic and straightforward. After each three-minute round, the bell rings and the busy activity in the gym falls silent as the boxers take a 30-second rest. Amidst this silence you can hear the harsh reality of the sport of boxing as primal noises pierce the stifling midday air; heavy breathing, guys gasping for air, snorts, grunts, groans. These are the sounds of self punishment, of dedication, of pain, of pure unadulterated hard work.

Twenty-year-old Dante "Chowking" Paulino attacks the heavy bag with a ferocity that speaks of raw rage. With his head tucked into his chest, he pounds the bag relentlessly. He hits with the power of a sledgehammer and does not let up for three minutes.

He is a good looking newcomer who's been a professional for just six months. With a broad back and heavy, toned muscles, he looks like a mini Mike Tyson. He fights as a featherweight—124 lbs.—and won his first two fights by crushing early round knockouts.

With no amateur experience, he came to Manila two years ago from Calbayog City, Samar, one of the poorest areas of the Philippines, wanting to be a boxer. He comes from a family of eight kids. Dad's a farmer and mom's a housewife. The family house is a small *nipa* hut near the beach.

"We're not poor," he says, "because we have three meals a day. My family wanted me to study, but I decided boxing's for me. I want to make something for myself."

He didn't know any gyms in Manila and in the meantime, he took up various jobs. One was as a prep cook at a Chowking fast food restaurant. One day he found the Elorde Gym and asked for a tryout. They put him into the ring and he barely made it through two rounds. He was rejected. He quit his job at Chowking and trained everyday for two straight weeks. He came back for another tryout and floored his opponent in the first round. Johnny Elorde told him to get his things and move into the dorm in the back. Because of Dante's previous job, Elorde dubbed him "Chowking."

"He's got a promising future," says Toti Sangalang, a long-time trainer in the Elorde Stable. Even though he's only earned a few thousand pesos in his first two fights, he says he's still focused.

"I'm after the fame and glory," he says. "Not so much the money."

Although Chowking is considered a prospect, the reality is, of course, that most who try their hand will end up with neither fame, glory nor money. To succeed in boxing in the Philippines, one has to not only be good, but also extremely lucky. A boxer has to be able to get a break, to get the big fights. The sport has been down for over a decade, with money for promoting and bigger purses scarce. Combined with the fact that literally thousands of hungry guys are fighting for this limited money, the odds of just getting beyond the status of a preliminary fighter can be extremely high. Still, though, they punish themselves. Six days a week, week after week, month after month.

Boxing could be the most difficult sport in the world. Many people who never see this side of the sport think that boxing is merely a matter of who can throw the hardest punch. That could not be further from reality. Boxing is an art, a science that has to be learned through grueling repetition. Just learning how to properly throw, say, a left hook takes hour after hour of practice, day after day, month after month. It can be mind-numbingly boring and painful, but it is the only way. Only then can a fighter learn to throw with proper leverage and balance, maximizing with precision his ability to throw punches that have the speed and power to destroy his opponent.

And, of course, boxing is more than just offense. A boxer has to always be conscious of defense, of protecting himself from his opponent's onslaught. Boxing can be compared to a violent chess match, where decisions have to be made instantly in the midst of explosive and grueling hand-to-hand combat. It's something that can only be learned in the gym. Jab-straight-hook. Just keep doing it over and over again, faster, stronger, better. No matter how much pain.

Trainer Eddie Ballaran works with a newcomer. With his bald dome, Eddie looks like a Filipino Yul Brynner. He wears boxing mitts on his hands while the newcomer wears training gloves. Eddie's training the young kid to throw a combination.

"Come on," Eddie yells, "jab, straight, hook." He holds up the mitts waiting for the boxer to throw the combo. The kid throws the combination into the mitts, and the collision makes a loud popping sound. He throws another combination and, again, it snaps into the mitts. But Eddie sees an opening. The kid's dropping his guard after throwing the first left. He goes for another combo but after throwing the jab, Eddie slaps the kid hard upside his head with the mitt.

The bell rings ending the round. The kid puts his hands down and begins to walk away to take the 30 second breather.

"Halika na!" barks Eddie, motioning the kid back towards him. "Jab, straight, hook." The kid is breathing heavily but does as he is told. He puts his hands up and throws the combo into the mitts. The kid is tired and falls off balance. Eddie slaps him on the back of the head with the mitt. Several other boxers who've been standing around watching start laughing.

On the wall over the entrance of the gym hangs a painting of the young Gabriel "Flash" Elorde, the legendary Filipino fighter whose eight years as junior lightweight champion of the world in the 1960's led to the creation of this building. He stands in the classic boxer's pose; gloves up, chin tucked, ready to strike. His painting serves as a reminder to all who enter of what it takes to become a champion and how a champion should live. The "Flash" was renowned for his punishing training regime. Fans admired him for that. But he also lived a life of humility. Fans adored him for that.

The Flash does not represent some unattainable legend, though. He was real. And the pictures hanging on the nearby wall of the other champions who have come through this gym remind the current crop that they, too, can reach the mountain top. But nobody's under any illusions here. Everyone knows the answer to making it is at once simple and difficult; pure hard work. Nothing more, nothing less.

Perhaps the cold reality of the sport is the reason why most boxing gyms are so stark and bare bones in appearance. There are no fancy exercise machines in here. Most of the training is done either inside of the two old rings, or on the floor. It's incredible what you can do with a bare floor and a mat. One boxer lies flat on his stomach and jerks his head quickly from side to side, strengthening his neck muscles. Several other guys lie on the floor doing various kinds of crunches, leg lifts, sit ups, all designed to harden the stomach.

On a bare patch next to the guys doing crunches, Raffy Montalban skips rope for 10 minutes without stopping. The 25-year-old from Bicol has seen many sides of the sport and has worked his way up to some success. He is the OPBF Jr. Bantamweight champion and is world rated.

He was a pro from 1989 to 1992 when he grew tired of the hardships of the sport and quit. For two years he

bounced around, worked in a gold mine, construction, making hollow blocks. Then his drive returned.

"I saw guys I knew winning," he says. "Then I wanted to come back." In 1996 he won the Orient title in Tokyo. He's defended it twice since. He lives in a small apartment in the back of the Elorde gym with his wife and two kids. To give you an idea of how tough boxing is, his biggest payday so far has been $8,000. He didn't have the time to enjoy most of it, though, because the money went to pay off a family debt and to pay for his wife's sister to go to college.

One cannot help but admire what Raffy and all these other boxers do on a daily basis. There are few endeavors that reveal so much about a person as boxing. Those who live a life of comfort do not reveal. Boxing reveals. "Can I make it? Can I win? Am I manly enough? Do I have the courage?" These are questions that are answered for all to see inside the violent and very public confines of the ring. As for the reasons why, all you have to do is go to the gym and listen to the sounds.

"I like the fact that it has been a massive learning experience in my lifetime," Paul said, "something most Americans will not experience. They don't realize how hard life is here. I respect these people very much. But I'll admit it. I'm a spoiled Westerner. I like not having to worry about spiders crawling into bed with me. I like not having to slaughter animals in the kitchen sink."

THE PRICE IS RIGHT

Paul Burns had had enough. He was frustrated and frazzled. And he wanted out of the Philippines, immediately.

For ten straight months this 43-year-old American had to put up with things that no man should have to put up with. He had snakes drop from the ceiling while he slept. Crazed turkeys trapped him in the bathroom. Witches visited him in the back yard. Many of his friends ended up on the dinner table. He often had to catch his own drinking water. He had not seen nor used any modern conveniences. And, oh yeah, after nearly a year of waiting, his Filipina wife still did not have her immigrant visa so she could travel with her husband to live in the United States.

"I don't ever want to see rice again for as long as I live," Paul said from his small rented apartment in Las Piñas, where I found him languishing with his wife Vic-Vic. We met because my wife happened to be friends with his landlord, who lived next door. When Paul spoke of his long lost life in America, he practically started salivating.

"I miss my crappy American diet. I miss my barbecued chicken cooked over the black jack oak. I miss my big refrigerator with thousands of snacks. I miss my cable TV, my aircon, the toilets that flush, all my appliances that work. I'll admit it. I'm a spoiled Westerner."

The distance between his home in Jacksonville,

Florida and his wife's family home in the poor farming village of Tapaz, Agusan del Sur, Mindanao is a long one, and not just in terms of miles.

"When I was a kid I was a boy scout," Paul said when asked to describe Tapaz. "I liked camping. I can camp for one week, maybe two weeks. But ten months living in the wilderness? No, not for me.

"Tapaz was like going back in time 150 years. When I first went there they were using *bolo* knives to open cans, which is dangerous, because my brother-in-law has a two-year-old daughter. So my second time back I bought them a can opener. They didn't even know what to do with the damn thing. They just sat there and looked at it. That's how far behind they are."

He and his wife came to Manila because they were told they had finally, mercifully, accomplished the massive amount of paper work required in order to get her the visa. But they were misled. When I met Paul there was no end in sight. Both the United States and the Philippine government seemed to have endless demands. His life had already been put on hold for nearly a year and he was very nearly broke.

"In Cuba, they were handing out US passports to any Cuban that wanted one," Paul said frustratingly. "I'm an American citizen. This is my wife. It's absolutely ridiculous." And to think this weird odyssey began with a measly two dollars and an advertisement in the back of a cheesy 20-year-old detective magazine.

Originally from Chicago, Paul had been residing in Jacksonville for 11 years since 1985 where, as he described it, he had been living an incredibly unexciting life. There he co-owns a pet shop and also works as a chef for a chain of chicken restaurants. He had been working six days a week. He worked nights and when he came home he would watch television until dawn, go to sleep, get up after lunch and then prepare to go to work again. He never went out and he never dated.

"I was comfortable in my boring life," Paul said. His business partner, however, began urging him to find a girl. "She said, 'You need an Asian girl.' I said 'Why?' And she said, 'Because you need someone who is super dedicated to her husband, who's a good cook, who will take care of you.' And I thought 'Yeah, I'm not getting any younger, I'm 41 years old. I don't want to die alone, so what the hell.'"

He had no idea where to start. He looked inside the closet and found the old magazine and the ad for a company called Japan International, which promised to bring together Asian women and Western men as pen pals. Paul sent in the $2 for information. They sent him back all the brochures.

"They were nice brochures," Paul said. "The company actually looked legitimate." He sent in the $35 sign-up fee. "What's $35? I figured I've got nothing to lose." Several weeks later they sent him back an information form. He had to describe himself and also describe what kind of girl he liked. He desired someone semi-young, attractive, long dark hair, a farm girl who enjoys music and writing. He sent in the form and then, several weeks later, he received a brochure with pictures of about a dozen women inside, whose bio-data fit his interests. There were girls from Japan, Malaysia, the Philippines and Singapore. He picked the domestic helper from Singapore.

"Vic-Vic's was the worst photo of them all," Paul said. "But for some reason I kept coming back to it. Hers was the odd ball photo. I had picked out three girls, including hers, and wrote letters to them. But I only mailed hers. After I dropped it in the mailbox I forgot about it. I never expected an answer."

Several weeks later he got a reply. It was then he found out Vic-Vic was a Filipina. He wrote back. She responded again. By the third letter he asked her to marry him.

"I didn't want to waste time," Paul said. "I wanted to know if she just wanted to be a pen pal or something more." Vic-Vic accepted. But her contract in Singapore did not end for another year. And besides Paul had never been on an airplane before. In the ensuing year they exchanged over 400 letters, sometimes writing twice a day.

Occasionally Paul would call and they would talk for nearly three hours. When Vic-Vic's contract ended in June the next year, Paul flew to Singapore to meet her and to take her back to the Philippines.

"It was like seeing someone I hadn't seen in a long time," Paul said of their first encounter. "We got to know each other very well through our letters." They immediately flew to Manila, connected to Davao, then on to Tapaz.

"I wasn't naive about the Philippines," Paul said. "I had done a lot of reading. But I didn't realize Tapaz would be that remote."

Nestled between the mountains of Agusan del Sur, about a half-day's drive away from Davao city, Tapaz is so remote that jeepneys do not even go there. The only public transportation in Tapaz is motorcycle taxis.

"If people want to go somewhere," Paul said, "they usually just hop on a carabao and go."

Nobody ever delivers mail to Tapaz and the nearest post office is a 20-minute motorcycle ride to the town of Josefa, where you will more than likely have to wake the postman from his deep slumber in order to get any service.

Once in Tapaz, Vic-Vic's brother and father grilled Paul for days about his intentions, his personality and what kind of job he had in America. Having satisfied the family, Paul and Vic-Vic were married a few days

later. This marriage between a Filipino and a foreigner
brought on the biggest party Tapaz had ever seen. Over
one thousand people turned out to celebrate. They
slaughtered three pigs and a huge water buffalo. A
disco was set up and they played, among other songs,
a warped version of Billy Ray Cyrus's "Achy Breaky
Heart." The wedding lasted for four days. Paul and
Vic-Vic left for a weekend honeymoon at the Paradise
Island resort and when they came back, everybody was
still partying. With his ticket about to expire, however,
Paul went back to the States.

"Suddenly I was back in the States alone again," he
said. "Psychologically it crushed us both." He came back
to Tapaz and vowed to stay until he accomplished all
the paper work in order to get Vic-Vic an immigrant
visa to go to America. He thought it would just be a
matter of filling out a few forms. It turned into a bu-
reaucratic nightmare. So he ended up living in Tapaz
for ten straight months.

In Tapaz, Paul lived in the family's small, simple
wooden house with no ceilings and a native nipa roof.
They had electricity but mostly at night only. There was
no glass on the windows and no interior doors. Rooms
were created by tacking up blankets and sheets. The
house was made of simple boards nailed together and
animals could easily get in. Snakes would drop from
the ceiling while Paul and his wife slept. Giant spiders
would crawl in the house at night. Sometimes big lizards crawled across his pillow. Rats, pigs and chickens
casually walked through the house.

"They get most of their drinking water by catching
rain water," Paul said. "If it doesn't rain, you don't
drink." There were NPA guerrillas in the mountains
and often times Paul could hear their gun battles with
the military. "At first I asked my brother-in-law if
that was a thunder storm and he said 'No. That's the

rebels and the military fighting it out.' I said 'Oh, is that all?'"

The last white man Tapaz's residents had seen before Paul was back in 1980. That guy worked in Tapaz at the banana plantation but could not stomach living there so he would retreat everyday to Davao and his air-conditioned hotel room.

"Everything I did drew an audience," Paul said. "When I took a bath at the village well, it drew an audience. I chopped wood, it drew an audience."

Everybody thought he was rich. "A little girl said to me, 'You're rich.' I said 'Why do you say that? And she said, 'Because you're wearing a ring.'" The biggest assault on his sanity, however, was the lack of anything to do.

"People are afraid to go out at night," he said, "because they're terrified of snakes and witches." Paul claims even he encountered a witch one night in the back of the house. "It scared the hell out of me."

He was so bored that he became close to many of the village animals, spending hours watching their silly antics and conversing with them. But the problem with this was that many of his friends ended up on the dinner table, which upset Paul greatly.

And it was not just that he was constantly losing his friends to the evening's menu, it was the way he lost them. Being an admittedly spoiled Westerner, Paul's idea of grabbing meat was to go to the refrigerator section of the supermarket and make a neatly packaged selection. In Tapaz, however, if meat was on the menu for dinner, they would just grab a turkey or a chicken from the backyard and slit its throat right in the kitchen sink.

Some of his closest friends were the obnoxious family turkeys, who along with the other village turkeys formed a gang which walked around terrorizing people.

Paul's turkeys used to chase people around the house and sometimes trap them in the bathroom. Because of their high-brow attitude, Paul named one turkey Tough Guy and the other Tough Guy Jr. Upon their gastronomical demise, however, Paul became rather unhappy.

"I was quite upset about that cantankerous, egotistical snooty old boob getting his throat slit," he said. "Tough Guy had a brain the size of a marble, but he and his rough neck band of hooligans added life and personality to the village. When they were gone, I was sad."

Back in Manila, he thought they were ready for the climactic interview with the official at the US embassy who wields the ever elusive visa stamp. The embassy, however, threw him another curve when it suddenly asked for a Singapore police clearance for his wife.

"I'm very frustrated with the process," Paul said. "The length, the time, the expense. And after you go through the entire process, they can still say no. The little wet-behind-the-ears punk sitting behind a desk in his air-conditioned office at the US Embassy can still deny you a visa. And then you have to go through the whole process again." The ordeal had its bright side, however.

"I liked the fact that it has been a massive learning experience in my lifetime," Paul said, "something most Americans will not experience. They don't realize how hard life is here. I respect these people very much. But I'll admit it. I'm a spoiled Westerner. I like not having to worry about spiders crawling into bed with me. I like not having to slaughter animals in the kitchen sink."

He lost 15 pounds, his nails were overgrown, his mind was still quite frazzled and his life was still in limbo. But at least Paul Burns now has a loving wife and a lifetime full of stories.

Thanks to an old magazine and a $2 gamble.

HER TRUE REFLECTION

She stood before the dresser mirror, brushing her long, dark brown hair. It was nice to have long hair now, she thought to herself, as the brush glided through her thick mane. Two years ago, just for a change, she had cut it all off after she had grown it down to her rear end. And now that it had grown back, she found herself looking forward to this time of day, the end of the day just before sleep, when she could stand in front of the mirror and brush it in long flowing strokes. It was like a ritual, something to meditate on, where as she brushed, the thoughts seemed to flow.

She told herself she likes the mirror. Well, of course, the mirror didn't lie. She did not like the few creeping gray hairs, and anyway, she thought to herself, what woman does not question something or wish she could change something every time she looks into the mirror. Maybe it was more like she was comfortable in front of the mirror. She had nothing to hide. And thus the mirror did not show her anything to feel upset about.

As the brush navigated the dark strands, pausing momentarily at the knots, she studied her brown skin in the mirror. Was she really too dark? Well, she wasn't fair skinned, that's for sure. Anyway, it was all so absurd. She couldn't believe her mother said that straight to her face today.

"You're too tan," her mother had said tersely and matter of factly over lunch at Megamall. "You should be lighter." There soon came another line about the way she dressed. The rubber shoes were ugly, as were the jeans shorts and the hair in a pony tail. It was as if Mom were disciplining a nine-year-old, instead of talking to a mature woman in her early 40's. Mom said she was ashamed of her daughter. Nearly directly implied that she wasn't fit to meet the relatives who were visiting Manila from the States. So she didn't go. But she knew the relatives would be wondering where their favorite cousin was and no doubt her mother would make up some excuse, and it wouldn't be about her daughter being too tan.

What was funny, and infuriating, was that her mother did not even bother to ask what she had been doing lately. Of course it could have literally been anything. Her car could've broken down and she had to walk three kilometers in the midday sun, she may have been on vacation down in Boracay, she may have stopped to talk to a nun in the street, something her conservative Catholic mother would no doubt approve of. Hell, it could've been anything. There could be 8,000 reasons why she was so tan. And what was so bad about being dark? Lord knows it was natural. She was a Filipina dammit! She tanned just by walking from the cab into the bank. But no, her mother didn't care about any of that real life stuff. Only that her daughter was too tan and that that fact alone somehow shamed the family name.

And this thing about the way she dressed was just as stupid. Her mother doesn't even bother to think that maybe her daughter was in a hurry and just threw something on without thinking about it, or that she might have been doing the wash or cleaning up the house this morning. Again there could be any reason, right?

Well, she surmised, her mother came from the old school where you always had to look your best. Her mother would never understand that sometimes there are advantages to looking different, to being under dressed, to having different faces at your disposal. For one, you do not get too familiar to other people. And also, you can go to so many more places and mix with so many different people than you might otherwise be able to if you always played it one way. It's nice sometimes not to be noticed. Well, they'd notice you, being an attractive woman and this is the Philippines, but they'd be surprised that you're among them, and thus you're more likely to get what you want. You don't always have to "impress" people and put on airs of morality and importance. You can get what you want in hundreds of different ways.

So many Filipinas only knew that one direction, she thought, as she dragged the brush slowly through her hair and watched herself in the mirror. There are so many who liked to play that game of status and money. They wear the latest designer clothes, use skin whitener, have a face lift, talk about their latest trip to the States and the hot, trendy restaurant in New York they've eaten at. Not so subtly reminding people how important they are because they're rich.

Well, that was okay when you needed it. Even though she was not anywhere near rich, she knew how to impress them with that angle if she had to. Put on the right clothes and jewelry, offer up good table conversation, nothing but the most impeccable manners and charm. But there were so many other directions one could go, so much out there that one could be.

The strokes through her thick mane became long and sweeping and she was in some kind of trance. She was watching herself in the mirror while she moved the brush, but she seemed to look right through herself.

Yes, she thought, her mother would never understand. But she learned early on that it was to her advantage to be able to have knowledge of as many different avenues in life as she could. At first it was probably by necessity. Her mother and father were ultra-conservative Catholics. Perhaps because she was the eldest of five girls, who knows, but they suffocated her with rules, depriving her of any kind of normal teenage life. They would not even let her attend the school dance at her high school in Manila, not even with a chaperone!

Her mind wandered back to that time nearly three decades ago when she made that fateful decision to do her own thing. Heck, anything to get out! At 20 years old she married the first one that came along. He was a handsome, dashing Filipino, he had been to the States and his family had money.

Together, they lived a decent life, had a nice house in Tagaytay and started a few small businesses. But he was spoiled. He didn't like responsibility. All he ever did was play with his expensive toys, while she took care of their kids and ran the businesses. And then he started abusing her physically. Threatened to shoot her with a gun. One time he even beat her with the butt of the gun. She hung in there for almost 11 years. Trying to do the dutiful thing. A Filipina does not leave her husband. Her mother told her that. No matter how bad things get, you stick by him. That's your obligation.

But she finally broke, had enough, took the kids and left with P43 in her pocket. Naturally she ran to her mother's house. Her father had already passed away and her mother had a house in Pasig. Her mother took her in but was disappointed in her daughter's decision. And her mother hadn't changed. She treated her daughter like she was an 11-year-old. If she came home too late, the gate would be locked and she would have to climb up and jump over the gate. How many times did she almost slash herself climbing over that pointed gate? Again her mother didn't even bother to ask where she had been, perhaps out trying to help herself and her children by getting a job, doing some schmoozing at some big hotel, anything at all. All her mother knew was that it was too damn late!

And so she left on her own, and moved into a one room box in some squalid barrio in Quezon City with the kids. Out into the cold, cruel world with the children. She did not want help from the family. They would've only held it against her. And certainly her ex didn't care and never sent the kids one peso. There were times when she didn't know how she would be able to feed her kids lunch. She thought she might have to sell her body just to get a few pesos. Fortunately she never gave in. And, somehow, she always found something for the kids and herself to eat. She lowered her expectations and learned to live from meal to meal. And she got by. She did different jobs, worked in a bank, a brokerage firm, buy-and-sell, getting what she needed and wanted. This is where she really learned the value of being different people, of different modes of dress, of having many faces. Out of a need for survival.

Her looks would attract all kinds of men and lord knows she could have had any one of them. Sometimes she would find herself having dinner at the Shangri-La or the Peninsula with some big shot businessmen and politicians. There were plenty of offers. One Filipino businessman wanted to marry her and promised her a house on the Italian Riviera and another in Aspen, Colorado. There was another rich guy who courted her who was fond of telling people that he had a home in Beverly Hills and that Frank Sinatra lived next to him, not the other way around.

But she had pulled herself through the worst of her ordeal, set herself and her children up in a decent rented house and educated them. Screw their money, she thought. Men were always trying to impress her with their money. She wasn't about to be awed by the glitter and the promises. They would have to do a lot more than wow her with money to win her over. She had strength, she wasn't that easy. She had to be tough.

She thought about her court case against her ex. After she got fairly settled she practically taught herself the law and sued, trying to get what was rightfully due to her. Ten years and it is still going on! Damn these male justices! Not one peso of support from her ex and the justices have held it up for 10 years. And there's never an explanation. Oh, these male justices were something, she learned that. She knew they slowed things down for her, denied her and her children any kind of justice.

"Maybe they wanted to molest me," she thought. "Maybe they hate me. Maybe they're just chauvinist old men who want a woman to die serving a man. Dammit, he pistol-whipped me! How can they call this justice?!"

She felt a bolt of anger shoot through her body. She pulled the brush in hard, bold strokes and it seemed to fly through her long hair. Yes, she had to fight, she told herself in a fiery trance, staring through her own eyes that blazed back at her from the mirror. She had to learn and keep learning, because it was essential for survival. Otherwise they would eat her alive. She wasn't born into privilege. And nobody ever handed her anything.

Then suddenly she saw her face in the mirror and she stopped brushing. It was as if the mirror had brought her back. Her heart was beating fast but her reflection calmed her and made her feel good. She liked this time of day and she knew why she liked the mirror.

"After all this turmoil, I'm still present," she said softly to her reflection as she laid the brush down on the counter. "I'm still standing in front of the mirror. And I still trust myself when it comes to the mirror. Because the mirror never lies." She leaned forward and stared calmly into her own eyes. "You have to be a woman of many faces," she thought. "I have to see what's going to happen at the end of the rainbow. I'm going to find out what's there. I'm fighting it out all the way."

She picked up the brush from the dresser top for one last go around. As she brought the brush to her long brown mane, she saw her reflection give a small smile back. It was a smile of contentment.

No Whine For The Canine

They stole our dog. I do not know who 'they' is, but it surely must have been some lowlife deluxe schmucks who snatched her and took her away. And in broad daylight.

When it happened I had just woken up from a rare and pleasant afternoon siesta. I remembered seeing Shiggy, our pure bred white spitz, in the garage doing her usual thing of scratching fleas before I went and dozed off. When I got up an hour and a half later, she was gone. I looked around the house for her and couldn't find her. I looked at our other dog for some clues, seeing as Shiggy is his mother. I call him Don Amigo Señor Eggs *Gago* (idiot). Eggs for short. Eggs because his brains are scrambled. His response was typical; that clueless face with the head tilted to the side. As usual Eggs was just looking for a handout.

I proceeded outside because sometimes the dogs slip under the gate and roam around near the house, looking to leave their special gifts for the neighbors to deal with. She wasn't there. I waited an hour for her to return with no result. I walked around the block looking for her and saw nothing. She never disappeared before. I knew right then that she had been taken and we would never see her again.

I immediately turned suspicious of everyone in the neighborhood. I thought of the young kids on the block who liked playing with Shiggy. A few days earlier they were petting her out in the street when one looked up and said to me, "Hey Joe, *aso*(dog) *adobo!*" All the kids laughed. I became a tad repulsed thinking about how casually people talk about eating dogs around here. But I knew the kids were joking and did not do it. Too innocent.

I turned my suspicion towards the tricycle drivers, who hang out at the little bakery across the street from our house. It's easy to suspect them, because they are never very friendly. These guys always strike me as a lower breed, perhaps lower than dogs. I recalled a jarring scene several weeks before when I saw some guys out catching dogs late one night on Sucat Rd., the main road which leads to our subdivision. I was driving by at about two in the morning on my way home. I heard the awful yelp of a dog, and quickly turned my head towards the cry. I saw a mangy brown mutt being scooped up inside a tricycle.

Of course, I couldn't have stormed over to the bakery and accused the trike drivers of taking Shiggy as they would simply have denied it. But I vowed never to buy any food from the bakery anymore. Some of the neighbors were hanging outside their homes and I asked them if they saw anything. They all shook their heads. But the old lady across the street assured me that our dog was alive.

"No, no, they didn't kill your dog," she said. "Pure breeds are not very good to eat. They make you hot inside when you eat them. If you're going to eat a dog, it has to be a street dog. So don't worry. I don't think they ate your dog. They probably sold it for P500." Gee, how wonderful, I thought. Thanks Grandmom. I could smell cooking food wafting out of her kitchen and I excused myself before she decided to invite me to dinner.

As I walked home, throwing a nasty sneer to the trike drivers, I imagined the horror Shiggy experienced when

they held her down and brought the knife to her throat
and the two by four to her head. I could imagine the
hideous cry of panic and pain she would let out. The
callous indifference of her captors and killers, who
would quickly perform the dirty deed, skin her, roast
her and then eat her. I imagined them having a big
party as they devoured their delicacy of our dog. The
little slimy creeps!

You should understand, however, that I was not
overly upset over the loss of our dog. Ever since I've
been in the Philippines, I've known the reality for
dogs here. I've always figured it's just a matter of time
before some hungry soul out looking for a feed happens to chance upon any old dog, and I guess this was
Shiggy's unlucky day. Perhaps I was more bothered by
the fact that somebody had come along and just stolen
her in broad daylight. Like any victim of a robbery, I
felt violated.

And frankly, I have never had an affinity for any dogs
in the Philippines. Philippine dogs repulse me. They are
wretched, mangy and dirty. They have that look that
comes from too much indiscriminate screwing around.
Most are basically street mutts who pass themselves
off as pets. They are good for barking at strangers and
letting you know someone is lurking outside. Most,
however, appear to lead tormented lives, scratching
and clawing at themselves all day. I find little to like
about them.

Yeh, I know. I should try being a dog in the Philippines and see how I like it. I should try sleeping in
somebody's dirty, mosquito infested car park night in
and night out. I should try living with vermin like mice
and endless parades of cockroaches and blood sucking
ticks. I should try existing in a world where some of
the big creatures think my flesh goes quite well with
San Miguel Beer. I have thought about all that and,

well, it doesn't sway me. Every time I have tried to feel empathy and sympathy for a Philippine dog, the emotion just dissipates. Probably had to go earn a living or something important like that.

For sure I never thought I would think this way. In the United States, where I come from, dogs are considered man's best friend. I used to love dogs. Had one of my own growing up and cried silly the day she died. Dogs in the States are treated better than people. People send their dogs to dog camps for recreation, serve them expensive yuppie dog food, buy them designer dog clothes, and talk to their dogs as if they are people and can understand.

The best description of how dogs are treated in America came from comedian Dick Gregory in the 1960's during the height of the Viet Nam war. At the time America was in turmoil, with many young people protesting the war and demanding it be stopped.

Gregory pointed out that most parents never questioned the military draft, as they believed sending their children to fight for their country was the patriotic thing to do. However, he cleverly observed, if the government started drafting people's dogs to go fight in Viet Nam, the entire country would be up in arms and demand an immediate end to the fighting. "They're drafting who Mildred? Little Spot here? Over my dead body! I think it's time we go march with them young hippies."

Third world reality can radically alter ones thinking, however. At one point we had as many as four dogs. Shiggy was a rather nice dog, would bark when a stranger showed up at the gate, but basically she was a horny slut. Her escapades with the brown mutt down the street left us with two more mouths to feed; Eggs and an ugly, orangish thing whom I named Pinakbet, because the color of his fur reminded me of the squash used to make one of my favorite Filipino dishes, pinak-bet. Then came Tiny, a miniature poodle given to us by my sister-in-law. Tiny was a cute, semi-wretched, crazy little thing who used to jump around in circles and crawl on the ground on her stomach. All because I would do something spectacular like walk out the door of the house to the car park and sit on the stoop.

Pinakbet was the first to go. He fell ill one day and just died. I wanted nothing to do with it. Au's cousin came over and put him in a big plastic bag and carted him away. Later I asked him if he had buried the dog.

"No," he said nonchalantly, "I threw him on top of a garbage dump somewhere in Las Piñas."

"He's just on top of a pile of garbage inside a plastic bag?" I asked, a little bit astonished.

"Yeh," he said with a casual smile, as if it was no big deal.

A few months later Tiny keeled over. I had been out of town and I didn't even notice her missing until a few days after I had already returned. "Where's Tiny?" I asked Au.

"She died," she said not even looking up from doing some paperwork.

"Died?" I yelped. "Just like that? You sound like you don't even care."

"Well I feel for it, but I don't make space in my brain for the dog. I've got too many things to think about."

Well, at least they did not just throw her body on top of a rubbish heap. They dug a hole for her in the dump and buried her there.

But it was Au's comment which really hit home. Yes, life in the Philippines. Survival is hard enough for the humans, so chaotic and crazy. Who has space left in their brain to think about the dogs?

Indeed this was her reaction when I informed her about Shiggy, whom she had bought for P2,000 as a baby. She felt for Shiggy but she just could not find the space in her brain to care for too long. Just another hard luck creature like ourselves, I thought, trying to survive in this dog-eat-dog, and, dare I say, human-eat-dog, world.

Don Amigo Señor Eggs Gago, are you paying attention?

A SPOT OF AFTERNOON TEA

Like any right proper Englishman, Alec stopped whatever he was doing at precisely 4 p.m. and settled down in the nearest café for his afternoon tea. In this case the place was the Delifrance inside the Robinsons Place mall in Ermita. By pure chance, I happened to be sitting at a table just behind him slurping down a bowl of corn soup when he turned to me and struck up a conversation.

He was a perfectly polite, elderly gentleman—75 he said—fairly rotund and dressed casually in tan slacks and a red checkered, short sleeved, button down shirt. Actually he was Welsh and he told me he owned a taxicab business back in Wales. He said he had never before been to the Far East. He had come to Manila with a buddy of his, Joe, who also owns a taxicab business back in the same town in Wales. They had just spent two weeks in Thailand and were planning on staying in Manila for two weeks.

"Where are you staying at?" I asked him.

"Some place over here called the Cherry Apartelle," he said in his thick accent. "A real dive. The rooms are tiny and don't have any windows."

"How did you end up there?"

"My buddy Joe's been here before. He said he wanted to save money. But a window wouldn't hurt, would it?"

"I think the Cherry is a short time joint," I said.

"They have three hour rates where you can, you know, bring your lady and do your thing."

"Yeh, it sure seems like it," he said laughing.

"Why did you decide to come to the Far East anyway," I asked him.

"A couple of weeks ago," he said, "Joe rings me up and says he's going to the Far East and asked if I'd like to join him. He's been here several times already. He says, 'Alec, as soon as you return from the trip, you'll be crying to go back.' I said 'What are you talking about?' He says, 'Just believe me you'll be crying.'

"You know I've been to the States. I've been to Canada. Last year I went to the Caribbean and I had a good time. I had a good time in all those places. But when I came back I wasn't crying about returning."

"He's probably referring to the girls," I said.

"Yes, that's it," Alec said. "My God, Joe never stops. We spent a week in Bangkok and that's all he could talk about. Every night he wanted to go to the bloody bars."

"And did you go with him?" I asked.

"He dragged me to a few bars. Oh they got loads of 'em in Bangkok. Some real pretty young things too. But I don't go for that type of thing. That's not for me."

"You mean you didn't get a girl in Bangkok?"

"Nah," he said rolling his eyes, "I don't go in for that. I can't be bothered."

"Why?"

"It's more trouble than it's bloody worth. I've been through all that already. I'm 75 years old. Who needs it? When I go on vacation I like to have a look around. I want to see the culture, to see how the people live. Perhaps go for a swim. Read a book. Have a nice meal. A pint or two of beer. That's all. Just relax. I can't be bothered messing around with girls anymore."

"Well how about a massage," I said. "Did you go for

a massage while you were in Bangkok?"

"Yeh my buddy turned me on one day. That was something. The girl had me all twisted and turned about. But no hanky panky. Just a massage."

"That was it?"

"Well one night he takes me to one of these girlie bars and he insists on getting a girl for me. Heavens she was a gorgeous young thing. So she sits down beside me and I buy her a drink. But it doesn't take a genius to figure out she's interested in more than a drink. So right away I told her I don't want to sleep with her. She said she didn't mind. Would you believe this girl has a real nice, expensive car? So the next day she picks me up at my hotel and we drive all the way down to this beach resort, Pallaya."

"Pattaya," I said.

"Yes, Pattaya. Oh we had a wonderful time. I spent a couple of days with her. We slept together one night, that's all. But no hanky panky. Mostly we went for a swim, had some nice meals."

"That must have cost you," I said.

"Oh you better believe it did. About $70 a day."

"And what did your buddy do?"

"He stayed in Bangkok and went wild. I tell you he really goes for this type of thing. Everyday since we've been here he's been with a different girl. In fact he's with one right now. Imagine that?" He pointed to his watch. "It's bloody 4:30 in the afternoon and he's got himself a bird."

"Where, at the apartelle?"

"No he drove out about an hour out of town. This one's an old girlfriend of his. I told you he's been here several times already. He met her the last time he was here. A young bird. I think he's in love with her for Christ sakes. He bought her a flat, sent her to school. He's even been sending her money. But I think he's got problems. I think she has another boyfriend." I laughed.

"That's been known to happen to a few foreigners over here before," I said. "A lot of guys come here and fall in love with the first one that comes along. Then they marry the girl thinking they just hit the jackpot with this beautiful young thing and the next thing they know they didn't just marry the girl, they married her and 29 of her family members. And then they gotta buy daddy a new carabao and a new *banca* boat." Alec laughed and shook his head.

"I told him he's got to be crazy," he said. "But he says, 'No Alec, I love the girl. She's so pretty and so sweet. I haven't felt this much passion in years.' Now we're about the same age, both in our 70's. I says, 'Joe, what's all this talk about passion? Guys our age aren't supposed to get passionate and lovey dovey. You're supposed to keep your head about you and just enjoy yourself.' But he says, 'But I love her.' Oh brother, I tell you. I think he's lost his mind."

"What have you been doing in Manila?"

"Well, I'm just having a look around. I don't go for all these girls. Like I said I want to see the culture. I want to see how the people live. I just went out to the market a couple of miles from here."

"What market?"

"I'm not sure what the name was. Something Bac or black ..."

"Baclaran."

"I suppose that's it. I asked the taxi driver to take me to the market. I like to go to markets. The taxi driver took me there. I looked around for about 30 minutes, bought a few things and then he drove me back."

"What did he charge you?"

"P450."

"P450? I think you got ripped off."

"Well right from the start he said it costs P200. He

pointed to the meter and said 'Look it's P200.'"

"No," I said, "at the start it costs P20 not 200."

"Oh heavens, I suppose I did get pinched, didn't I?"

"And you're in the taxi business, imagine that? I think you should get out of Manila and go to an island."

"Well Joe said he'd take me down to one of the islands. He said you have to take a ferry to get there."

"Oh good then you'll see the real culture. How about tonight, is he taking you to the bars?"

"Yeh, he wants to drag me to the bars. But I like to play cards. Blackjack. And I play a bit of the wheel too. He said there's a casino down the street from here. But right now I'm going over to this other hotel just down the street, where I'll talk to the manager and arrange to have a swim."

"Well Alec," I said shaking his hand as I stood up, "it was nice talking to a gentleman such as yourself. And nice meeting you."

"Yes," he said standing up from his chair, "and it was a pleasure meeting you. A right way to spend a half an hour, wasn't it?"

"If I win, I go to the palengke *(market). If I lose,
I have nothing."*

WITH EMPHASIS ON THE WORD "FOREIGN"

It never fails. One minute I'm cruising along thinking everything in the Philippines is "normal." Normal
as in, it's just like where I come from; the fancy cars,
the cable TV, the modern malls, the English speaking
populace, the English language newspapers, the pro-
liferation of American schlock like fast food joints and
cheesy Hollywood action movies. I'm lulled into a sense
of complacency, of thinking that I'm back home living a
life no different than I used to in the boring suburban
bedroom community of Allentown, Pennsylvania where
I grew up. Then, like a snap of the fingers, something
comes up, bites me in the butt and says in a deep au-
thoritative voice, "Yessiree son, you are definitely in a
third world country, a very foreign land, with emphasis
squarely on the word "foreign!"

It's a combination of the almost casual violence,
the outrageous scenes and the weirdness I encounter
which, while certainly nothing exclusive to the Philippines, seem to happen awfully close to home in the
Philippines and with a certain regularity. Check out
these examples which happened over the course of
several months; my wife saw a man run over by a truck
in broad daylight in the Evangelista area of Manila.
A taxi driver told me the story of a foreigner who was
stabbed dead by another taxi driver, his friend, over a
P40 fare. I had my bike stolen. I saw that giant pig take
a pee and a crap in the middle of a busy street. A guy

I knew as a casual friend was brutally murdered up in the province town of Tarlac. I rode the SuperFerry boat the night it almost capsized—and three days before the Princess of the Orient liner went down. We flew Cebu Pacific down to Cagayan de Oro one week before the same plane crashed in the mountains. I was crossing the street and a punk riding a bicycle the wrong way slammed into me. (He fell to the ground and got hurt, not me, but it stunned me, nonetheless).

Still no matter how much happens, I get complacent. I guess because I prefer the easy road in life and I tend to pull the wool over my own eyes. In other words I like slack. I try to take the slack wherever I can find it. And lord knows there is plenty of slack to be had in the Philippines.

And so after all of that had happened, I had taken the slack and slipped back into that "normalcy" mode. Probably because I was doing "normal" things like attending the noisy birthday party at Jollibee of my wife's one-year-old niece, dealing with cleaning our apartment, the cheesy videos I watched of giant lizards about to eat us all and an asteroid ready to obliterate the planet.

Then one Wednesday afternoon the fun began anew. I walk into the office of some Filipino friends of mine in Parañaque. I visit there regularly as I often work with them. I happen to be in the neighborhood and merely want to say hello and see what's up. As soon as I walk through the door to the office, I see a crowd of people hovered in a circle in the back room. They look like they are attending to someone who's been hurt or had a heart attack.

"What happened? What's going on?" I ask the secretary.

"It's Salvador," she says in a matter of fact tone. "He is possessed by an evil spirit."

"A what?" I say, more than a little surprised. "An evil spirit? What do you mean?"

"About an hour ago he collapsed," she says. "So they called a faith healer. He's now trying to take out the evil spirit inside Salvador."

"Why didn't somebody just take him to the hospital?" I say.

"No he's already been to the hospital," she says. "He also collapsed before about one month ago. When he went to the hospital the doctor said they could find nothing wrong with him." I walk to the back of the office where the small crowd is gathered. A yellow candle burns on top of a nearby desk. I look inside the crowd and see the victim, Salvador, lying on a couch, his eyes closed. Hovering over him is a short man in a T-shirt, baggy black pants and sandals. He is Brother Ding, the faith healer.

Brother Ding is busy at work. He waves his hands over Salvador, he leans close and talks to the evil spirit, he raises his voice and yells at the spirit, he whips Salvador with an old rag, he invokes the name of Jesus Christ, he massages Salvador's arm, he presses one finger into the top of Salvador's head, he rubs baby oil on Salvador's midsection. All the while, Salvador remains calm, his eyes still closed.

Around his neck Brother Ding wears a cross, a pyramid with one eye in the middle and a small amulet I cannot make out. On the table next to Salvador sits the office altar consisting of a big wooden cross with the hanging Jesus, statuettes of Jesus and Mary and a small painting of Mother Mary and the baby Jesus.

Several times Brother Ding takes an unlit match stick and presses it into Salvador's fingernail. Each time he does this, Salvador, his eyes still shut, bolts upright on the couch as if the match were blazing hot.

"What does that mean?" I ask one of the office em-

ployees. "Is that really a hot match?"

"No it's not," the guy says. "But the spirit thinks it's hot. That means the spirit is still inside him."

According to the secretary, Brother Ding said the evil spirit possessing Salvador is a woman named Andrea. The story goes that Andrea had been raped and murdered by the Japanese during World War II in the exact area where the office now sits. Apparently Andrea was terribly jealous and possessed Salvador's body because she wanted him to marry her.

The guy then informs me that several people claim they have seen a white lady ghost in the building on occasion, specifically inside the ladies toilet.

"Myself I have not seen anything like that here," he says smiling. "But that's what they say." I consider that perhaps these women mistook the foul odor in the ladies' room for being a white lady ghost and that maybe somebody ought to call a plumber instead of a faith healer.

The clock reads a minute after three o'clock in the afternoon and somebody switches on a small TV sitting on top of a nearby file cabinet. The first picture on the screen is the bizarre scene of condemned rapist Leo Echegaray being led through a gauntlet of crazed photographers and bloodthirsty gawkers on his way to his imminent execution. It's the Philippines first execution in over 25 years and it looks like we might be able to catch it live on television. Several people in the office immediately turn their attention away from the exorcism and focus on the screen. There is some excited discussion about whether we'll see the actual execution live and in color.

"What is going on here?" I say. "You have an exorcism in the office and an execution on the television. You mean I can watch an exorcism and an execution at the same time? Can someone tell me what planet I'm

on?" Those who hear me laugh. Then someone assures
us that the scene on the television is just a video tape
and that Echegaray is being put to death at that exact
moment. The television is then switched to cartoons.
The exorcism resumes its place on center stage.

What strikes me is the nonchalance of nearly everyone in the office. It seems like any old day. There are
several incoming calls. People stop by to drop off a pack-
age or to pick up a letter. Most who wander in walk to
the back and watch the proceedings for a moment, turn
around to do their business, then go on their way. For
those who work in the office, they spend a few minutes
watching Brother Ding work on the evil spirit. Then
they go back to doing whatever they do, like updating a
ledger or reading a proposal. After a few minutes they
turn their attention to Brother Ding. It's as if they are
watching a repairman fix the copy machine.

Yes, just another day at the office. As if it's a perfectly
normal thing for the secretary to lean over and say,
"Excuse me Mr. Lerner, Johnny's possessed by an evil
spirit." In the same manner she would lean over and
say, "Excuse me Mr. Lerner, you have a phone call on
line two." And then I say, "Ok hon, I'll take care of it in
a minute." Nothing outrageous. Just normal everyday
procedure.

After nearly an hour, Brother Ding proclaims Salvador free of Andrea. He proves this by sticking another
match stick in Salvador's fingernail. Salvador doesn't
budge. However, he still lies on the couch with his eyes
closed. Brother Ding tries to revive him. He then calls
for some charcoal. Somebody runs out and brings back
a dish of black charcoal and lights it up.

"The smoke will ensure that the spirit will leave the
room," says the secretary. The office quickly becomes
filled with thick smoke, which ensures that I leave
the room. As I exit Salvador is still lying on his back

with his eyes closed while Brother Ding tries to revive him.

Good story—right? Well wait, it gets better.

Later that night I am at home recounting this tale to my wife when I hear a sickeningly primal sound which appears to be that of two dogs having a vicious fight on the street outside. Ever the gawker, I walk outside to catch the spectacle of two dogs tearing at each other's flesh and trying to kill each other.

Once out on the street, I walk towards the vicious growls and quickly discern that they are coming from the neighbors' house. The neighbors have iron bars surrounding the front porch and I quickly notice their dog, a fairly nice healthy white and brown mutt, in the bushes by the bars. It appears that the dog has his head stuck in the bars and is panicking in trying to pry himself loose. I get a better angle and notice two guys, one standing on the porch and the other standing out in the street. They are holding a cord and the cord is wrapped tightly around the dog's neck. All the while the dog writhes, jumps, squirms and howls hideously. A handful of people are standing around watching the proceedings.

"What's going on?" I ask one old man. "Is he alright?" The old man drags his finger across his neck and shakes his head.

"*Pulutan*" (drinking snacks) he says. Then he laughs. "No just joking. They don't want the dog anymore so they are taking it to another house. They are trying to put the dog in that big blue bag."

"Why do they have to put the dog in a bag?" I ask.

"Because he does not want to go?" the old man says. "They are trying to calm him down." The two guys holding the cord continue to pull hard. The dog yelps furiously. He has his mouth wrapped around one of the iron bars. Then I hear several loud cracks and am sure that they have just broken the dogs' neck.

"Hey Joe, you eat dog?" says another old man with a big smile.

"Yeh right," I say, "*Aso adobo*." They all laugh. "Nahh not me," I say.

"Some people in the Philippines like to eat dog," the first old man says. "Not me. It burns the insides. I like to eat lamb." I play along but I know what's up.

Meanwhile the dog has been subdued and placed inside the blue bag. Then a man on a bicycle with a sidecar attached pedals up to the house. Normally he sells vegetables in the neighborhood by day. The two guys dump the dog inside the side car.

"What are you doing with the dog?" I ask the lady who owns the dog.

"I don't like it anymore," she says, "it smells bad. We're giving it to a cousin in Tarlac." As the *gulay* (vegetable) man peddles away with his latest offerings, Lynlyn, the four year old daughter of the lady, collapses to the ground and starts crying for her dog.

"*Na ko!*" says the mother, brushing off her daughter's howls. As I shuffle back home, I feel a pain on my butt. Then I hear a deep voice and it utters a familiar refrain: "Yessiree son, you are indeed in a foreign land, with emphasis placed squarely on the word 'foreign!'"

They Play The Sport Of Survival

The Philippines has never won an Olympic gold medal. Two silvers in boxing, five bronze including boxing as well as various other sports, but never gold.

Filipinos, though, can take solace in the fact that there is one sport in which the Philippines could very well sweep the gold, silver and bronze if it were offered as an Olympic competition. That sport is pool or billiards.

Unquestionably pool should be in the Olympics. Heck, they consider shooting an Olympic caliber competition. And like shooting, pool is simply a supreme test of hand-eye coordination.

Probably the main reason a sport like pool is out and shooting is in is because of image. No matter that pool is currently the fastest growing participatory sport in the world. Pool cannot seem to shake its reputation of a game played in smoky bar rooms filled with hustlers, gamblers, low-lifes and non-workers. And for Juan Antonio Samaranch, the president of the International Olympic Committee, it's all about that squeaky clean image. In his mind, pool probably does not fit the Olympic ideal, whatever that is.

Which is not to suggest that the surly reputation of pool is not well deserved. But there is also another side of the story. Like top competitors in every sport, world-class pool players put in countless hours of practice, dedication and sacrifice to become the best. Look at Filipino world champion Efren "Bata" Reyes. He has dedicated his life to pool and, as a result, has become a living legend worldwide. Through billiards, he has lifted himself and his family out of poverty. Surely he deserves a shot at Olympic glory.

Until the day the Olympic people come to their senses, however, Filipinos will be denied a chance at proving they are the best. And Filipinos are truly some of the best pool players in the world.

On the United States Pro Billiards Tour, Efren Reyes wins regularly and is considered by nearly everyone associated with the sport to be one of the greatest pool players of all time. Francisco "Django" Bustamante also wins regularly and was ranked the number one player in the world in 1998. Rodolfo Luat, Jose "Amang" Parica and Leonardo Andam have won various tournaments, are always highly competitive and are always considered a threat.

These five Filipino players make up the Philippine national team, a group put together by Filipino businessmen and brothers Jose and Aristeo Puyat. The Philippine team won the 1993 world championship in Nine-Ball, defeating the American team in Las Vegas.

Throughout the nineties Filipino players have performed so well, they have taken the game by storm. Their talent and skills have now become the standard by which other players worldwide measure their games.

"Americans invented pool, but Filipinos mastered it," said Edgar Acaba, the 41-year-old president of the Philippine Cue Artists Association, and himself a professional pool player for 18 years. "I think the Americans don't want Filipinos to come to the States to play anymore. They're getting jealous because

Filipinos are taking over the game."

How a third world country like the Philippines became a pool phenomenon is often a mystery to outsiders. However, those living or spending time in the country are hardly surprised. In the Philippines there are perhaps more pool players per capita than in any other country on earth. And these are not just hackers out to pass the time and drink a few beers. There are legions of excellent Filipino players.

Billiards was introduced by the Americans in the early part of the century and Filipinos took to the game naturally. The game seems to fit the Filipino temperament perfectly; it is laid-back and ideal for gambling. Billiard tables are hidden everywhere in the Philippines—inside run down canteens, down every back alley, on street corners in teeming barrios, in the many modern bowling and billiard halls throughout Manila. And the tables rarely lack for action. Many who have nothing better to do—and in the Philippines there are plenty of them—spend their every waking hour on or around the pool table.

One reason Filipinos are so good at pool is that not only do they play often, they regularly play "Rotation" and "Nine-Ball." Although "Eight-ball" is the most widely played pool game worldwide, Rotation and Nine-ball, along with straight pool, are considered the true tests of pool. Rotation especially, which is the game of choice amongst everyday players in the Philippines. What makes Rotation so difficult is that all 15 balls are on the table at once and they have to be run consecutively. The heavy traffic of balls means that the player has to develop excellent creativity.

However, the main reason Filipinos are so good at pool is that for many in the Philippines, billiards is not just a pastime. It is literally their life.

"For Filipino pool players, it is our bread and butter,"

said Bert Aleonar, a professional I befriended at the Coronado Lanes in the Farmers Plaza shopping mall in the Cubao area of Manila, where, in the mid 90's, many of the best pool players in the Philippines gathered nightly. "If we don't win, we don't eat."

This is the literal truth. It is a matter of their daily bread. Boy Ducanes, a 44-year-old who's been playing professionally for 20 years and supports a wife and one child, put it quite succinctly when he said, "If I win, I go to the *palengke* (market). If I lose, I have nothing."

This is not the case for the Japanese, the Taiwanese, the Germans and the Americans, who also excel at pool. They are not as hungry, so to speak. And because Filipino always play for money—money that might feed their families—they have become better under pressure than many of their counterparts from around the world.

"They don't practice," Efren Reyes once told me when I asked him why Filipinos were so good under pressure. "Their practice is gambling. A lot of pool players don't have jobs. Their job is playing pool."

"Gambling is our good training," said Acaba.

At "Farmers," one could regularly see this uniquely Philippine phenomenon in action. While the scene has since spread out to various pool halls throughout Manila, for several years in the mid 90's, Farmers was the Philippines' best pool hall. Every night, Monday through Friday, this modern bowling lanes cum billiard hall was crowded until one, sometimes two in the morning, with various professionals, assorted wannabes, trick-shot artists, gamblers, hangers-on, and others who love the game with a passion. When "Bata" Reyes, Bustamante, Andam and Luat were back in the Philippines, they often dropped by to play.

"Here at Farmers," Bert said, "you have the best card players in the Philippines, the best pool players,

the best gamblers, and the best *cristos* (bet takers)."
(Interestingly, you will notice that the word "hustler"
has not been mentioned. That's because that old art
is strictly frowned upon and those who practice it do
not frequent Farmer's or any other well known pool
hall where professionals hang out. A person caught
hustling will probably wish he never showed up. Sort
of an unwritten rule).

One does not have to travel to the States and play in
major tournaments to be called a professional. Anyone
who makes his living playing pool—and registers with
the government's Games and Amusements Board—is
considered a professional. Acaba noted that there are
more than 50 registered professional pool players in the
Philippines with about 32 being of world class caliber.
However, the number who regularly earn their daily
bread by playing pool could easily be in the thousands.
There are also hordes of good amateurs. Jorge Dacer, a
46-year-old professional whom I met at Farmers, said
there were probably 30 guys at the time who could
compete with "Bata" Reyes in Nine-Ball.

At a pool hall like Farmers, sometimes the pros will
play the pros. Since most of the professionals rarely
have their own money, they become like hired guns.
They have to find a financier or a sponsor. Guys usually
just show up at the pool hall with their cue case slung
over their shoulder and no prearranged match. They
might have to wait for several hours but eventually,
they may find a financier and an opponent.

The average bet for a match between two professionals is P3,000 to P5,000 Bigger money matches from
P10,000 up to P200,000 and beyond are not uncommon.
The split can be 50-50 or even 70-30, with the financier
taking the larger share.

There are also plenty of decent amateurs with money
who want to challenge the professionals for big money

games. Often times they are well-off businessmen who love pool and love to gamble. These matches can often be difficult to arrange because the amateur always wants a handicap and the financier of the pro naturally does not like this.

Handicaps are also given in matches between two professionals. The extent of the handicap depends on the level of the opponents. "Bata" Reyes is considered unbeatable in a straight up match of Rotation. Every professional taking on Reyes in Rotation will ask for a handicap, which comes in the form of having to score fewer points to win the game.

The matches are either Nine-Ball or Rotation, with the winner being the player who first reaches the agreed upon amount of games. As at most pool halls, there are several signs posted at Farmers that read "Gambling Strictly Prohibited." Regardless, people gather around the table and openly bet on the matches.

"You can't stop gambling," said Leopauldo Vincencio, a nightly observer of the Farmers scene. "In billiards, you have to have some money on the game. If not, it's not interesting." Before the match, the spectators around the table place their bets. On a busy night, there can be more than 50 people watching. Cristos walk around looking for guys with money. They offer odds. Guys flash hand signals—three fingers flashed sideways indicates P300—and then they point to their bet. Just like at the cockfights. There are side bets on individual games. Everybody watches quietly and intently. They follow each shot. After each game money changes hands. Everybody pays up.

One man acts as a spotter or referee. Why a referee?

"Because Filipinos will do anything to win," said Jorge. "If they know they committed a foul but the opponent didn't see it, then they won't say anything."

On the other side of the coin, though, the players look after each other. The winner will always make *balato*—giving his losing opponent some money, usually P100 - P200, so he will not go away completely empty handed.

If he gets on a few hot streaks, a good pro can earn perhaps P20,000 - P30,000 a month playing money games. But as in so many professions in the Philippines, the real money lies abroad. There is no pro tour in the Philippines. According to Jorge, there were, during the mid-90's, ten Filipinos in Japan competing in pool, six in the States, and two in Taiwan.

Filipinos are clearly some of the most sought after billiards players in the world. As a sport, billiards is exploding worldwide and many tournament sponsors are looking for the best talent. There are also foreign financiers with money who are always on the look-out for good players. Generally a player will get known through word of mouth, say, from having performed well in local tournaments and having played at Farmers or one of the other big pool halls with other pros. He then might get invited for a tournament in Japan. The invitation secures the visa. But once there he will stay for a month or two, using his cue stick to try to earn some money. There are always money games with people looking to take on a pro, with a handicap of course. As is the case back home, the Filipino will need a financier as he never plays with his own money. Rarely does he have any money of his own. The life can be a struggle.

"I heard some were even sleeping in the sauna bath in Japan because they had no other place to stay," said Jorge. He did not have to worry about where to stay. He is a well established professional. He has been a professional player since 1978. Pool is how Jorge makes his living. He has no other means of income.

He showed me an invitation written entirely in Chinese, inviting him to come to Taiwan for an upcoming Nine-Ball tournament. This would be the fourth time he visited Taiwan. After playing in the tournament in Taipei, where first prize was $7,000, he was to hook up with his Taiwanese friend and financier who owns a billiard café in Yuan Lin, a town about 300 km away from Taipei. There he planned to hang out for at least nine hours everyday. He would be available to give lessons to the customers and also take on anybody who wants to compete against him. Of course, they play for money. He stays at his Taiwanese friend's house and receives a salary from him.

Then a few months after his Taiwan stint, Jorge was planning to travel to Hamburg, Germany at the invitation of his German financier, Andreas Rohr. Jorge was planning to stay in Germany for maybe six months. That would have been his fifth time in Germany. Rohr owns a billiard café and Jorge works at the café as the resident professional. There are also weekly small professional tournaments which Jorge enters. He is quite well known in Hamburg and he often takes first place in the local tournaments. He once won the German Open Nine-Ball tournament. His financier covers his room and board and Jorge said he can pocket P20,000 a month which he sends back to support his family in the Philippines.

"We know we are the best in the world," Jorge said. "But the people here don't care. Especially the sponsors. The only sponsor who cares is Puyat." However, the Puyat brothers cannot reasonably be expected to sponsor every prospect who comes along. Indeed the amount of good pool players far outnumbers the amount of sponsors willing to finance a good player. Boy Ducanes spent eight months in Taiwan as a professional in 1990. Since then, however, he has not been able to find another sponsor and has not been able to go back. He has had to earn his living on the tables in Manila.

"We have a bright future in pool," said Edgar Acaba. "But we need the support of the government." However, there is no government money or program supporting Filipino pool players. And with pressing priorities, such as trying to feed and shelter the country's millions of poor people, there probably won't be a program any time soon.

Which means that the large contingent of aspiring pool greats from the Philippines will continue to be on their own. The rest of the pool world, however, shouldn't count on this cold fact from stopping the Filipino players. Even with very limited backing, Filipinos have, through hard work and dedication, firmly established themselves among the world's best in the sport of pool. Against nearly impossible odds, that is undoubtedly an incredible feat. Perhaps one day the world will see the master cue artists from the Philippines rewarded with gold around their necks. That is, if the Olympics finally wake up.

WHERE'S MY CHRISTMAS?

There's a popular saying at Christmas time in the Philippines that goes simply, "Where's my Christmas?" No matter where in the Philippines you travel, you are constantly greeted with that seasonal phrase as it is chanted like a mantra by the needy, the less fortunate and, of course, the opportunistic.

"Where's my Christmas?" they say, and you are expected to hand over some coins or bills. Well, maybe I should've been asking the very same question because we literally missed Christmas. We had just returned to Manila from a trip in the States and left Hawaii the afternoon of December 24th. We flew right across the international date line and arrived in Manila late Christmas night. Of course, the Christmas spirit, and the inevitable question, were still everywhere one looked.

I exited the plane dazed, parched and blurry eyed. The way you get when you've flown 12 hours across a wide ocean in a plane with stale, recycled air with only three hours of holiday booze-induced sleep the night before. I stumbled into the baggage claim area, picked up two luggage carts and found an open space next to the carousel. While waiting for the bags to come rolling up the conveyor belt—which surely would be crammed with record amounts of *pasalubong*-laden *balikbayan* boxes—I excused myself, told my wife I'd be right back and headed towards the men's room. Inside stood a young, smiling attendant.

"Hello sir. Merry Christmas sir," he said politely. I gave him a nod, not quite able to figure out his purpose here. Actually I've never been quite sure of the purpose of bathroom attendants anywhere. Just what is their function? To relieve you of the incredibly arduous task of retrieving your own paper towel after you wash your hands? To make the harsh, smelly reality of a men's room more humane and polite?

I knew, however, that this guy's presence had something to do with him hitting me up for something. I stood at the urinal and did my thing, then quickly washed my hands. I could see him lurking off to the side with the paper towel in his hand. As I wrung my hands he handed me the towel, sparing me the indignity of performing such a highly complicated and degrading task by myself.

"Thank you," I said.

"You're welcome sir," he said, smiling. "Where's my Christmas sir?" Frankly I wasn't in the mood to get hit up for his "Christmas."

"Uhh, err, yeh—Merry Christmas to you too," I said, also smiling, as I tossed the paper towel in the trash and walked out. I suddenly realized that everyone from here to the street would be smiling, nodding, blowing smoke, holding doors, complimenting me on how wonderful I was and how terrific the foul plane odor rising off my tired body smelled all because they too wanted their "Christmas."

Back at the luggage carousel I was loading our bags onto the carts when a young guy wearing a "porter" shirt approached my wife.

"Merry Christmas ma'am" I heard him say politely. "Can I help you with your bags ma'am?"

"Hmmm," I thought. "Where the heck was he just a minute ago when I was loading all the bags?" Well,

I was too dazed to really care. He won the job of cart pusher and got behind one of our heavily loaded luggage carts. I pushed the other one. Through the "Nothing to declare" lane where the customs lady let us right through, into the lobby, past some sign-holding people wishing me the best of the season,—if I only stayed at their hotel—out into the street and over to the taxi stand where some smiling men and their Tamaraw FX taxi were waiting for us.

There were something like five guys helping us board the Tamaraw. One guy held the back door while the porter loaded the luggage. Another held the side door for me. The other three just stood around. None of them asked for their "Christmas," but I knew what they were thinking. Each one had that "Where's-my-Christmas?" glow on their faces. Maybe with all the big bags I was carrying, combined with the few extra inches I had around my waist from too much holiday eating, it appeared that good old St. Nick was in their very presence. All they got from me, though, was a jolly old "Merry Christmas!" and a wave good-bye. I handed the porter two dollars.

"Merry Christmas, sir," he said, pocketing the money.

The driver drove us through the dark and empty streets to Sucat. The deal had been P250 but I gave him P350 instead. Not a bad tip, I thought, for helping unload a few bags. He seemed disappointed as he folded and pocketed the money. Not even a "Merry Christmas" from him.

It was the next morning, Saturday, the day after Christmas when the onslaught started. Well, it wasn't exactly an onslaught, but it was kind of interesting, nonetheless. It's incredible how fast word spreads around here. It must have been the talk of the neighborhood back in November that we left for the States.

And now that we were back, well, word spread like an Indonesian wildfire that we had just returned.

Now, I'm very aware of the duty of one who travels outside the Philippines to return with *pasalubong* (gifts). Naturally we had plenty of that in our still unpacked bags. But the pasalubong was for family, friends and people whom favors would be required of down the road.

And believe me when it comes to "their Christmas," I take care of my people. Not that I employ anyone on a regular basis. But I know who's who and who gets something on the holidays. Funny thing about the people who traipsed to our door that day; I never recall having much of anything to do with any of these people throughout the year. And hey, didn't they all realize how darn expensive the States can be and that we came back pretty much broke?

First up was the old carpenter. Once earlier in the year we hired him to build us a table. It was early morning when he came sauntering up to the front door. I was wondering what he could have wanted, seeing as we had just arrived the previous night. He last worked for us like eight months prior. For sure we didn't owe him anything. Oh, but of course. He was looking for his Christmas.

"Christmas?!!" I shouted when my wife told me the old man's purpose. "For what? What did he do for us? What does he do, go around to everyone he's ever said hello to in the last year and ask for his Christmas? Did you give him anything?"

"No, are you kidding me?" my wife said. "I told him to come back in January and that we might have some work for him."

They kept coming. Two little kids I've never seen accosted me out in the street. They didn't exactly ask for their Christmas, but they sure had that look on

their face. I just smiled. Several bicycle pedicab drivers
lurked outside our front gate waiting for "their Christmas." One driver yelled to me as I walked outside, "Hey
boss, where's my T-shirt?" Was I obligated to give this
man, whose name I didn't know, and whose services I
hardly ever used, a Christmas gift?

"Uh, yeh, how ya doin', next time," I said. That's gib-
berish for 'forget it.'

Several of the neighbors brought over holiday foods
and said hello. This was a nice Christmas touch and
soon our kitchen table was filled with Filipino foods.
Then the neighbor lady who lives three doors down
shuffled over and asked my wife bluntly, 'Hey Au,
welcome back. Where's my gift?' She's a boorish lady,
and I can't ever recall having much of a conversation
with her. Sometimes her daughter and my daughter
play together. That's the extent of our contact. Au
brushed her off with a comment about how we were
still unpacking.

Later that afternoon, I saw her coming in the front
gate to our building and she said, 'Hey Ted, Merry
Christmas. Where's my gift?' She caught me by surprise. I was caught in that zone that so many foreigners
get in where I suddenly wasn't sure about the appropriate local customs. Was it mandatory that I have
something for my neighbor, even though I have said
maybe six words to her in the year that I have known
her? Is it the foreigners' duty to give and not receive?

"Uh, err, uh," I said. "I dunno. Maybe you should
talk to my wife. Yeh right. Merry Christmas." I dodged
that bullet. I went inside and started talking to myself,
imagining she were still standing before me. "Where's
your gift? Your gift is that you are privileged to have
such a fine neighbor such as myself! Are you happy
now?"

For the next week I continued to dodge her. Every

time I saw her coming I suddenly had to run inside to urgently do something that I didn't really have to do.

Amazing how you get hit up from the weirdest angles during the holiday season. The night after we arrived we went shopping at the duty-free store near the airport. Afterwards we were riding in a taxi and as we drove up to the exit, the guard stood up, walked out of his shack and flagged us down. The cab driver stopped and rolled down the window. The guard signaled for the entrance slip. I'd done this trip more than a few times and knew the system. Taxis don't get entrance slips at the duty free store because they don't park in the lot.

"We didn't get a paper," I said. But of course the guard knew that that was the system. He looked in at us and said 'Ok Merry Christmas.' He just stood there for a moment as if waiting for something. He was looking for his Christmas.

"Sorry boss" I yelled from the back, "I missed Christmas this year."

MY CENTENNIAL JOURNEY

The great thing about all the Philippine Centennial celebrations in 1998 was how effortlessly and in so many ways one could celebrate the Philippines' declaration of independence. Even without realizing you were celebrating anything. For it seemed everything one did those days, even the most ordinary of activities, had Centennial written all over it.

If you happened to be out, say, shopping for a new dining room set, you could get a discount at a Centennial Furniture Sale. If the muffler fell off your car, you could buy a new one at a Centennial Muffler Discount Price.

You could also slurp on a Centennial Slurpee, eat a Centennial cheeseburger and Centennial *baboy* (pork), store your leftovers in Centennial containers, adorn your body with Centennial perfume, receive Centennial discounts when you dialed overseas, go to certain salons and walk away with

a Centennial Cut, drink your Centennial bottle of San Miguel, smoke a Centennial cigarette, get married and automatically earn the right to be called a "Centennial bride" and even become Miss Philippine Centennial and earn the moniker—get this—"Filipina for the next Millennium!!" (You'd think up until the bicentennial would have sufficed.)

Now while you, as I, are no doubt perplexed as to what exactly cheap mufflers and revolution have to do with one another, it is clear that the Philippine Centennial was one of those can't-miss marketing tools. Not unlike when the Pope came to Manila. Remember the TV commercials?

"His Holiness' visit to the Philippines is being brought to you by Jollibee! And by Magnolia ice cream!" However, like the visit of the Pope, the Philippine Centennial was also much more than just a way to hock burgers. The Centennial also provided a very real and fascinating historical marker. Whatever one did and whatever one saw at that time was how the Philippines looked exactly 100 years after declaring independence. That may seem like a fairly obvious statement but still, it's true. The Centennial was a moment frozen in time. (A Kodak Centennial moment, no doubt). Good, bad, beautiful, ugly. It was what it was—the culture, the people, the events—and that time will be remembered that way 100 years into the future, when Filipinos and the world will be celebrating the Philippines' bicentennial.

It is in this celebratory Centennial light that I now present "Ted's night-time Centennial Trip down Roxas Boulevard." Why Roxas Blvd. and why at night time? Well, Roxas Blvd. is unquestionably one of Manila's premier avenues. And there is a heck of a lot of action and entertainment there. Just the amount of neon alone makes this stretch of road worth a look. Sure, it's not the strip in Vegas or the Champs Elysee in Paris. But if you're looking for excitement, fun, laughs or just a good feed, you can do pretty good for yourself on Roxas Blvd. And besides, I happened to have a pretty interesting night there right around the time of the Philippine Centennial celebrations.

My Centennial trip down Roxas Blvd. began not as such but more out of curiosity. I have been to all kinds of places on Roxas Blvd. before, but there is so much I hadn't seen or done. There are so many places with giant neon signs that seem to promise so much. What's behind all those bright lights that I pass so often, I wondered?

The catalyst behind this trip was the presence in Manila of my Japanese friend Masa, who decided to take a breather from his overly stressed-out life in Japan and pay me a visit for several days. Masa likes to describe himself as a "ridiculous Japanese." He has a bit of hippie in him. Sprinting through train stations like the rest of his countrymen never quite appealed to Masa.

We began our journey in a taxi cab with absolutely no specific destination other than Roxas Blvd. This was how the entire night would go. We didn't take a trip. Rather, the trip took us.

The fun this evening begins in a small "disco theater" called the Black Stallion, which enticed us inside with a half-lit neon sign of a giant horse standing on its hind legs. Promising horselike virility, no doubt. The heavily discounted entrance fee helped too.

We are sitting at a small wooden table watching a bored-looking brunette in her early 20's dance in her bra and panty to a song which an alien from outer space might mistake for this country's current national anthem: "Barbie Girl." The song is fast, silly, catchy, junior high schoolish and utterly campy. And it's probably the most popular song in the land. The Centennial chart buster.

"I'm your Barbie girl, in your Barbie world. Wrapped in plastic, it's fantastic!"

The girl is moving at less than half speed to the music, almost in slow motion. As if she has just drunk a bottle of glue.

"Come on Barbie let's go party. Touch me here, touch me there, hanky panky."

The place looks about a quarter full. We are the only

foreigners around. We are being attended to by an overly attentive waiter named Eddie, who won't stop talking.

"Remember, I'm Eddie. Eddie, your waiter. Don't forget now. I take care for you. Okay? I take care for you, you take care for me. Whatever you need, you let me know. Okay, don't forget now. You need another beer? How about a pretty girl? Don't forget now. Eddie, the waiter, Okay?"

Several tables are occupied by Filipino guys either drunk, haggard or ogling the dancer. At one table, a guy is asleep in his chair. At another table five guys sit around a dozen empty bottles of San Miguel, while one has his arm around a girl. That's his Centennial bar girl. And that's her Centennial ladies' drink. Several other tables are occupied by sleeping waiters.

The Black Stallion is a classic cabaret bar right out of the 1960's with a large ground level dance floor surrounded by the audience on three sides. It has the usual mirrored disco ball turning around and the multi-colored neon disco lights blinking on and off. A string of lights hung everywhere on the ceiling looks like a lighted snake moving quickly around the room. On the wall behind the stage in big letters reads a sign, "Nonstop Entertainment." Indeed.

"You can touch, you can play, you can say I'm always yours."

The girls come out one or two at a time, dance two songs, take off their clothes down to their bra and panties, then leave the stage for the dressing room. Every single one of the girls wears a blank or bored look on their face. One even comes out and looks pissed off. All the dancers look pretty under the bright lights. But one saunters to the front of the stage and I can see she's wearing half a kilo of makeup.

All but one moves so slow to the music that you could

hardly call it dancing. That one who danced fast still had the bored look, though. They all just sort of sway. One pair comes out and does a simple set routine of steps in unison, but they do it in what looks like slow motion. The girls dance to disco tunes, love songs, the latest silly club songs. Many of the songs are by the same group that performs "Barbie Girl."

"If you will be my king, wooohoooo, I will be your queen, woooohooo."

The name of the group is called Aqua. They sound like a funky Abba. Their music consists of catchy, super-fast, ultra-techno dance songs with some of the most totally inane and ridiculous kiddie lyrics ever put out. This is the music three-fourths of the country is waking up to these days like it's the morning national news. This is how Filipinos get through another day of washing clothes by hand.

He sings, *"I am your candy man ... coming from boun-tyland."* She sings, *"I wish you were my lollipop!"*

It's so silly, so campy that it's actually good. But what really won me over to this music was when I heard that the song "Barbie Girl" got Mattel, the company that makes Barbie dolls, really ticked off.

"Roses are red, violets are blue, honey is sweet but not as sweet as you." My God, this blows away anything Madonna ever put out, like "Material Girl."

She sings, *"Be happy!"* He sings, *"Come on let's go get it on."* She sings, *"Be happy!"* He sings, *"Everybody let's go have some fun."* I know these lyrics because I own the tape. Bought a bootleg copy for P50 in Baclaran. But back to the Black Stallion.

At one point the DJ introduces the cast. The girls come out and line up in one row across the stage. Each is now dressed in street clothes. Each one still wears the same bored-looking, blank, stone face from before. As their name is called they step forward a few steps, show themselves by turning around, then get back in line. Masa wonders why he isn't seeing any skin. I call over Eddie.

"Hey Eddie, I thought the girls take all their clothes off?"

"No, not at this time. You know we just had the elections. We still do not have a proclamation of the new mayor. Once we have the proclamation then everything will get back to normal."

In entertainment terms the dancing and show are pitifully awful. No sizzle, no pizzazz, dead dancing, and dead faces. If this were Las Vegas or Paris, the audience would have been hurling rotten fruit onto the stage.

But this is not Vegas nor Paris. It's Manila. And truthfully it is superb. Superbly bad. Like the music in here, the whole tired scene has reached that level of badness where it has crossed the line into being good. So bad it's good. Like a true B-movie which is pure, honest, glorious, unadulterated cheesy schlock. Nobody could ever honestly think up something like this. It just happens by pure chance. And actually Masa and I are having fun. Eddie the waiter can't do enough for us, the beers are only P35 a pop and they even handed out hot towels, which Masa, being Japanese, appreciated very much.

We have seen the whole lineup so we decide to exit. And besides, "Barbie Girl" has just come on for the third time in an hour.

"Thank you very much sir." Eddie says, following us to the door. "*Arigato*. Remember me. Eddie. Eddie the waiter. At your service sir. Next time I introduce you to a nice girl. Thank you sir. Remember Eddie the waiter."

It is just past midnight and within seconds of our exit we're inside a cab. I decide to move the entertainment

upscale,—"legitimate" you might say—and direct the
taxi driver to go to the Hyatt Regency. The Calesa Bar
inside has live bands. But when we arrive at the Hyatt
a few minutes later, the doorman informs us that the
band has just finished and the bar is closing. Oh well.
Can't say we didn't try. So it's back to the bawdy action.

In mere seconds we're inside another taxi heading
down Roxas Blvd. I direct the driver to Vixens, a popular girlie bar. We pull up and my door seems to open
mysteriously by itself. We're met by a midget, or rather,
a guy with his feet attached to his torso.

"Good evening boss," he says with a bright smile.
He's the "official" greeter at Vixens. The area outside
Vixens has some of the hardest core collection of "gap
fillers" in the Philippines. Guys who have created work
for themselves simply by appointing themselves to the
job, even though no job really exists. They simply make
up employment out of thin air.

Roxas Blvd. could be Manila's gap filler capital. You
especially find them hanging out on the parallel service road sitting under trees, selling single cigarettes,
operating portable canteens and working the crowds
who patronize the local businesses.

Around Vixens the gap fillers are thick. Each is on
hand to try and extract a little money out of the hundreds of foreign guys who patronize Vixens nightly.
For instance, both sides of the service road here are
packed with cars and every couple of spaces belongs
to the watch of someone else. With just a few parking
spaces to work, each gap filler can earn enough in one
night to feed his family for the next day.

The torso man has filled one of the most lucrative gaps
on the block. He works the space between the taxi and
Vixens front door where, no doubt, a lot of transactions
go down nightly. Most of these transactions involve for-

eigners who are either new to the Philippines and have no concept of the peso—so they give some to anyone who says hello—and/or they exit the bar completely sloshed and in a hurry to get back to their hotel, so they hand out P500 notes to some poor looking local in a raggedy T-shirt who simply waves down a taxi that was waiting there anyway.

It is Saturday night and Vixens is going off. The place is totally packed with foreign guys, mostly in their 40's, 50's and 60's. Perhaps they should call this place Viagra's, not Vixens.

The bar is dark and lit up mostly by neon and black lights. The focus of the men's attention is the stage where nearly 50 women in bright bikinis, all looking like tens, gyrate back and forth to the throbbing disco tunes. Is that Barbie Girl? But of course it is!

Masa is totally agog as we weave our way through the hyped throng to the back bar. It's too noisy to tell him that what he sees may not be what he gets. You see, black lights are the secret behind the success of these kinds of bars. A black light makes every woman look awesome, like a ten. It only seems to work for the women, though. The men still look old and drunk. Black lights also make anything white look electric. Like everybody's teeth, eyeballs and those with white shirts. Combined with everything else, it gives Vixens the air of an ultra-modern, wild disco. Pure decadence and then some. But really, it's just guys looking for their Centennial shag.

Most of the women on stage carry a dumb, absent-minded look on their faces. This is obviously different from the bored looks over at the Black Stallion because here at Vixens, the women are very likely to cash in tonight. The men carry on like there's no tomorrow. Hoots and hollers can be heard above the music. Many of the men look to be window shopping. Many look like they'll be taking the plunge tonight. And most will probably wake up in the morning, roll over, their head throbbing like last night's music, take a look at the young lady sleeping next to them and say through heavy beer breath, "Hey, what happened to that good-looking broad I went to bed with?" Not all will say this. But most will.

After a couple of beers, Masa and I are dragged out onto the small dance floor by two girls in street clothes. We dance to the latest pumping dance tunes including many from Aqua. The best tune, though, is the "Disco Titanic." Imagine that? A disco version of Celine Dion's "My Heart Will Go On." Dancing the night away as the ship sinks into the frozen ocean with 1,500 people headed toward their watery graves, while bikini-clad girls offer themselves up to anyone with P2,000. What planet am I on?

I leave Masa with his new friend and head off to the comfort room. There is a line outside the men's room so I slip into the ladies' room which is empty. On the floor sit several blood-red sanitary napkins. As I exit the ladies' room, I look at the decadent scene around me and wonder if any of these guys have been inside the ladies' room to see what I just saw. What might they think? Would they care after a day long drinking binge? And don't these girls ever take a night off?

I have lost my appetite—surely, you understand—and I inform Masa we're headed out. As we reach the warm night air, I notice he has his girlfriend in tow.

"Taxi sir?" I look down and see the torso man smiling at me. There are several empty taxis waiting but it's his collar. He opens the taxi door, I slip him a P20 note and the three of us climb inside. It's 2:15 in the morning.

"Where to?" the driver asks.

"*Derecho*," I say. "Grand Boulevard Hotel. We're going

to the casino." In the two minutes we are inside the taxi, I discover that the girl's name is Sprinkles and that she comes from Negros. She also looks incredibly ordinary. Perhaps the taxi should get a black light.

We soon arrive at the casino and have to let ourselves out of the cab. No torso man here. At the entrance to the casino we are required to pay P100 each, which Masa happily hands over. I have never failed to see the irony of paying an entrance fee for the right to piss away all your money. The casino calls it a qualifying fee.

"What does this qualify me for?" I ask the ticket lady.

"It qualifies you to go inside and gamble," she says with a smile. It's little things like this that make the casinos in the Philippines, at times, some of the most hateful places on earth. Oh, I'm under no illusions. Casinos make money and the customers always lose it, no matter where you are in the world. But casinos are supposed to go out of their way to make sure the customer feels good about losing his shirt. Give the gambler something in return like cheap drinks, cheap and tasty food, good entertainment.

I don't gamble regularly, only small amounts when friends are in town. But I see what goes on here. Casino Filipino must have the worst payoff rates of any casinos in the world, they have high minimum bets on the tables, the slot machines are the lamest anywhere, they charge outrageous prices for some of the worst food in Asia, there's no entertainment and the smoke level is as thick as the ocean is deep. If you can see past these faults—and, honestly, I don't give a rip—you can have some fun. Who doesn't like to pull a few one-armed bandits every now and then? And for sure the characters who hang out at casinos are all time.

It is 2:30 in the morning when we climb upstairs to the casino. The place is mobbed. Every table is packed with players surrounded by throngs of watchers. At least three quarters of the people are smoking.

Masa and Sprinkles head for the black jack table. I notice a thick crowd gathered around a large baccarat table. I walk over and see one old Chinese man sitting at the table alone and playing a hand. There must be 100 people watching him play. The man has a stack of about P200,000 in chips sitting in front of him.

"He's won five straight hands," says a guy standing next to me. The old man bets P50,000 on one hand. His cards add up to nine and he wins. He does this three times in a row. A buzz runs through the crowd, which gets thicker by the second. Everybody wants to know the man's secret. What has he got that they don't? I want to tell them that the answer is money, but I keep quiet. The old man wins two more times before finally losing a hand. He gets up to leave. That's his secret.

Masa's up, he's down, he's up, he's down, he's down some more. He's chain smoking and nervously tapping the table. Sprinkles stands there watching with a bored look on her face.

I walk through the throng looking for some good people watching, parting the smoke as I go. The crowd consists of a lot of older people, mostly Filipinos, a lot of Chinese Filipinos, several Arabs and a handful of white guys. People are betting all kinds of amounts. From P200 up to P10,000 and beyond. I don't see one person who looks happy. Actually they all look like they've been through torture recently.

The habits of gamblers are fascinating to check out. At the craps table, the guy with the dice performs the same elaborate routine each time he rolls the dice. He's trying to roll the number six. Before each roll, he picks up the dice and turns one to the number two and the other to the number four and places them exactly side by side. He then pats the table two times, blows into his

hands and then gently rolls the dice off the side wall.

Baccarat in the Philippines elicits one of the strangest habits in gamblers. After the dealer deals two cards face down, the players never just pick up the cards to see what total they have underneath. Instead, everyone puts their head real low to the table where they literally destroy the cards by bending them at the corner to see what they have. Baccarat is a simple game that requires no strategy whatsoever. Hiding your total is meaningless. I suppose, though, that it makes people feel like they're big shots when they can put on their poker face.

Masa and Sprinkles find me watching baccarat. Masa's got a handful of chips. He's up P3,000. I have no idea how he did it and don't ask. We immediately head off to the slot machine area. Along the way we pass the small dining area. There's a sign on the wall that reads, "Absolutely no smoking or sleeping." All the tables are occupied with people either smoking or sleeping.

In the slot area the noise level gets cranked up. Bells, whistles, coins dropping into metal trays. It sounds like everyone here is getting rich. Maybe we can too? Since Masa's here we employ the unconventional kamikaze method. Don't stick to one machine thinking that the next pull will bring four golden *calesas* and the P5-million prize. Hit and run. Just keep moving around, dropping coins into any machine that you pass. Sooner or later you'll find one or several that are hot.

It doesn't take long before we have money flying out of the machines. Fifteen coins at P5 each, then 30, even a hit for 150 coins. This could be our lucky night so we go for the kill. We cash in the P5 coins for P10 coins. Again we employ the kamikaze method. We hit, we run, we drop them in at random, we pull with excited anticipation and then, we look down with eyes and mouths wide open. We're broke within 30 minutes. All of Masa's winnings plus P2,000 more and P1,000 of my own money. A donation to the nation's Centennial.

We stumble out of a still very crowded casino into the light of dawn. It's 5:30 in the morning. We walk over to the Aristocrat restaurant and take a table by the window. Ah yes, the Aristocrat. Sure they've lost a step over the last few years, but, heck, the place has been around nearly since the time the Philippines declared independence. We order *sinigang na hipon*(sour soup with shrimp), Java rice, a cheeseburger, a Spanish omelette, *buko*(coconut) juice and Cokes. As we eat like starving wolves, I marvel at our selection of food. A perfect representation of everyone involved in Philippine history 100 years ago. Perhaps somebody is trying to tell me something.

As Sprinkles falls asleep with her head on the table and Masa chain smokes Mild Seven cigarettes while repeating, "This place is unbelievable," I look out the window at the street hustlers still working an angle— "Cigarettes? Juicy Fruit? Parking space?"—and, in a stay-up-all-night morning funk, it suddenly makes sense.

The new president of the Philippines will be known as the Centennial President. It's been said that he has a taste for the very kinds of activities that we just engaged in. Thus, our expedition straight down Roxas Boulevard at night could very well indeed be considered the perfect trip for the times in the Philippines. A real and true-to-life Centennial journey.

After over four years in Manila, Ted Lerner, along with his Filipina wife and their three year old daughter, moved 85 kilometers north to Angeles City, the former home of the American military at Clark Air Force Base. After one year in Angeles, however, he says he's seriously thinking about returning to Manila.

"Puroresu, Kampai!!"

The mild fall day has turned chilly as darkness settles over the stadium. The overflow crowd of 50,000 could not care less, however. There is a building rumble as they rise in excited anticipation. On the field a forklift has emerged from a tunnel carrying the object of their lust; a folded up, ten foot high barbed wire cage. Crewmembers remove the cage from the forklift and begin assembling it around the mat in the middle of the field. Piece by piece the cage rises.

The workers check every last detail. They tighten bolts and make sure all the wires are connected. Reporters and photographers are told to stand behind a line that has been placed around the cage, so as not to get hurt by any explosions. Two television cameramen don head to toe fireproof suits.

Suddenly the lights around the cage are turned on. The song "Wild Thing" blares over the stadium speakers as the announcer introduces Atsushi Onita. The crowd erupts into a frothy, passionate roar, a guttural din that sweeps the stadium. Tens of thousands sing in unison; "Wild thing!... you make my heart sing...!" Onita emerges from his locker room, surrounded by his entourage. He is greeted by an impossibly loud roar.

He walks purposefully down the aisle and towards the cage. Wailing cries of "Onita! Onita!" can be heard amongst the thunder. Fans reach out to touch him, as if he's a god. Cameras flash all over the stadium. Onita climbs the steps and enters the cage. The stadium seems to shake.

Without missing a beat, the announcer introduces Onita's opponent. A hard driving heavy metal song starts up and the crowd explodes again. Genichiro Tenryu emerges from the locker and quickly walks towards the cage. Chants of "Tenryu! Tenryu!" sweep the stadium. It is hard to tell who is more popular, Onita or Tenryu. Tenryu climbs through the door of the cage and the stadium becomes a bloodthirsty mob with the primal feeling of anticipation. For the Japanese fans, the intense pressures of their daily lives are suddenly meaningless. The only thing that matters to this howling throng is the fate of these two men, Onita and Tenryu, their heroes, their idols, locked inside a sadistically booby trapped, barbed wire cage. It is a monumental earth shaking battle happening before their eyes. A passion play of real life giants.

The door is shut and locked. It's time for Onita versus Tenryu in the Electric Dynamite, Barbed Wire Cage Death Match!

The other man inside the cage is the referee, who puts his ski goggles in place and signals for the match to begin. Onita and Tenryu immediately square off in the center of the ring with each one trying to throw the other into the barbed wire. A lady in her thirties near ringside is standing on her seat yelling, "Tenryu-san! Tenryu-san!" The crowd is on its feet, howling from the depths of its collective soul. It is an explosive and cathartic mix of fear and excitement as they hang on every move.

For ten minutes Onita and Tenryu work each other over with body slams, arm bars, figure four leg locks and some exciting near pin falls. Then Onita misses a move and goes flying into the barbed wire back first. The cage makes a huge explosion and the crowd screams. Onita just lies on the cage as if he is stuck. Then he collapses to the ground.

Several minutes later Onita, his top torn and blood spilling from various cuts, is on the offensive. Then it's Tenryu's turn to hit the cage. Another hideous explosion and the crowd goes wild.

The match stays fairly even for twenty minutes. Onita hits the cage one more time with another violent explosion. Just afterwards Tenryu slams Onita onto the mat, pinning his shoulders to the ground. The crowd chants to the referee's count. "One! Two! Three!" and Tenryu gets the victory.